The Science
Of Table Tennis

Brian Burn

ENGLAND TRAINER/COACH 1974–76

PELHAM BOOKS

LONDON

First published in Great Britain by
PELHAM BOOKS LTD
52 Bedford Square
London WC1
1979

© 1979 by Brian Burn

ISBN 0 7207 1155 X

Filmset in Great Britain by
Northumberland Press Ltd, Gateshead, Tyne and Wear
Printed by Hollen Street Press, Slough
and bound by Dorstel Press, Harlow

To John on his 21st birthday

Lots of love

Roxanna & Alan

The Science of Table Tennis

Acknowledgements

Table tennis is a very complex game that requires a great deal of understanding if one hopes to produce the best players. Behind every successful player there are always many people who work very long hours yet obtain little mention when the awards are presented.

When writing this book there were also many people who gave invaluable assistance and without their help it is probable that the book would not have developed in such a coherent manner. Mr N. Yazowa, a Japanese table tennis coach, gave excellent advice on the latest style of the Japanese and Chinese national players. The Malaysian Government's Sports Medicine Association were very helpful in allowing the author to attend some of their lectures on Sports Medicine, Sports Injuries, Physiology and Hygiene. Mr M. S. Firth of the British Cycling Association gave some very simple direct advice on the same subjects.

A few words of gratitude must also go to the Physical Education lecturers at Culham College of Physical Education, Mr D. Sykes, Mr R. Forsyth and Mr G. Dixon, for their invaluable assistance in developing the writer's knowledge of Physical Education while taking a specialist course from 1969 to 1972. Mr R. Farley M.Sc., a lecturer in Physical Education at the University of Petroleum and Minerals, Dhahran, Saudi Arabia, was also very forthcoming with advice regarding certain aspects of physical training.

Dr J. Josephson, Mr M. Collins M.A. and Mr V. Stevens B.A. gave invaluable guidance regarding the fluent reading of this book.

Finally, I would like to thank John Richardson, Alan Morpeth and Harry Dignan for all their help and coaching when I started to play table tennis at North Shields Y M C A.

To my wife, Linda

Contents

Modern stroke play
The forehand push; The forehand counter attack; The
forehand flick; The forehand smash; The forehand
topspin loop drive; The forehand topspin sidespin
loop drive; The forehand block; The forehand drop
shot
The backhand push; The backhand counter attack;
The backhand flick; The backhand smash; The
backhand topspin loop drive; The backhand block;
The backhand drop shot
The forehand backspin; The forehand topspin lob;
The forehand topspin sidespin lob
The backhand backspin; The backhand topspin lob;
The backhand topspin sidespin lob

The service
Aims of the service; Deceiving the opponent; General
body movements when serving

The return of service
Aims of the return of service; Footwork for the
return of service
Forehand attacking players; Backhand attacking
players; Defensive players

Strength tests
Physical Fitness Strength Index Test

Endurance tests
Harvard Step Test

Motor ability tests
Western Motor Ability Tests; Vertical Jump Test;
Table Tennis Test – Mott and Lockhart

Basic fitness tests
Static flexibility test; Dynamic flexibility test; Softball
throw test; Leg lift test; Cable jump test; Balance test

Table tennis report on an international player

**Planning a year's training schedule for table tennis
players**
The pre-season training period; The competitive
period; The post-competitive period. The annual
circuit of training

Warm-up activities; The ready stance; Terminal
positions; Follow-through; Stabilisation; Force;
Summation of forces; Work; Weight; Centre of
gravity; Angular motion; Conservation of angular
momentum; Mechanics of spin

Elementary standard of play; Intermediate standard
of play; Advanced level of play

**Techniques in coaching as related to skills in table
tennis**

Organisation of individuals, Groups and mass coaching

Illustrations

The majority of the illustrations in this book which show demonstrations of technique, training and exercise are photographs of the author. Almost all these photographs were taken while he was coaching in Malaysia and when he was Trainer/Coach to the English Table Tennis Teams during the 1976 European Championships in Prague, Czechoslovakia.

Introduction

Table tennis, like any other sport, is an educational process demanding psychological and physiological attributes. The first chapter is an introduction to the learning of the game.

There follow three main stages in this book. The first stage deals with stroke development for match play. The second stage is concerned with being physically prepared for match play and the third stage with coaching players for a match situation.

Stroke development progresses from basic stroke play to consistency of play and finally to advanced stroke combinations. All the strokes have been described in detail, but in the Advanced Stroke Combination section most of the emphasis is on the attacking game, which is used by the majority of the world's leading players.

Many players never reach their true potential because they are physically unprepared; yet in top table tennis, fitness can account for about 30 per cent of performance. If a player cannot move into a correct position to play a stroke, either through lack of power, flexibility or endurance, then his game is bound to be affected. Special consideration has therefore been given to how to prepare the body to cater for all aspects of physical fitness.

Many players do not achieve a good standard because they are coached wrongly either in stroke production or in their mental attitude. Successful coaching depends on the ability of the coach to explain the modern techniques and gain the respect of the players, so special attention has also been given to developing these equally important aspects of the game.

1 Basic Skill: Acquisition of, Development of and Transfer to the Playing of Table Tennis

When playing table tennis, it is essential that one learns the most effective way of developing skill. The essential quality is to have insight into the required strokes and to be able to visualise all aspects of them, so forming a kinesthetic image (see Chapter 9). Then one must place the complete picture of the particular stroke into one's own game. Insight can be analysed as a process where a player may look at a stroke in a detached way and not just be obsessed by his goal. It is not good enough just to watch someone smash a really hard forehand and then be happy to be able to hit the ball as hard oneself, so that it goes on the table. One needs to appreciate the importance of each movement of the body beforehand, during the actual stroke and in the follow through, as well as the position of the body relative to the speed and direction of the ball. Apart from the player having the ability to analyse a skill, he must also make sure that the person whom he is copying is demonstrating the stroke correctly. If one has good insight, it will help development, and the knowledge gained can be transferred to one's own game. If one can learn to discipline oneself in normal working life, then it is likely that thoughts and behaviour on the table can be controlled. Many good table tennis players wishing to progress have learnt new methods which have failed to improve their performance because their insight into the learning of techniques is not adequate. To improve this insight, different theories of learning have to be studied and this is precisely what players and coaches should concentrate on.

Learning can occur through the formation of conditioned responses, but if the environment is slightly changed, a correct response does not occur. If a player learns to push a 'floated ball'* so that it returns every time to the other side of the table he has achieved this by learning, but if a heavy backspin push is then used by an opponent and the receiver uses the same push stroke, he will put the ball in the net. This means that learning involves more than conditioning, and psychologists have extended the use of the term 'conditioning' to include not only elementary reflexes but also any 'complex of movements' which is in process at the time when the stimulus occurs.

One can learn a stroke by a method of trial and error, but this will always

* A ball that is returned with little or no backspin.

take far longer than being taught correctly. The more frequently a stimulus and response are associated with each other, the more likely it is that that particular response will follow the stimulus. Therefore one has to practise in order to learn a skill. One cannot simply observe others and hope to perform the same skill without practice. So the well-known saying 'Practice makes perfect' is very evident if one wishes to acquire the kinesthetic image.

Making table tennis strokes with good technique involves very complex skills and in complex skills, wrong responses are more likely, at first, than correct ones. A player must acquire a type of feeling of movement and touch to accompany a stroke. The 'Law of Effect' states that 'A modifiable bond' (between stimulus and response) 'is strengthened or weakened as satisfaction or annoyance attends its exercise'. A player must remember not to get annoyed because more than likely this will detract from his concentration. Sheer repetition of strokes, unaccompanied by feeling, is not likely to have much result. Learning processes depend on rewards and satisfaction and correct knowledge of results. When learning strokes it is always a good idea to introduce the notion of a target so that if the player achieves his task effectively, he gets the feeling of reward or satisfaction. Players with poor techniques fail to find satisfaction because there is no sound basis for progress. So it is important that the player should get as near as possible to the correct stroke right from the beginning. Once a poor technique has been developed, further progress may entail a complete change and involve more difficulty than the original movement would have. This is because a bond has occurred between a stimulus and a response and this 'pathway' is difficult to alter. This means that if a player is used to stretching for a ball he then finds it difficult to learn how to get his feet into the correct position. If he cannot do this correctly the player could become dissatisfied and unhappy.

Before one learns a technique one must assess one's capabilities, such as maturity, strength and flexibility. It is no good for a really obese person playing a table tennis game to try to cover all angles of the table with his forehand loop drive because his physique will not allow it. He would be more likely to succeed at a crowding, blocking game over the table.

When practising, the player should be encouraged to respond to the stimulus in the way in which it is desired and the stimulus should never be presented when there are chances that some other response will occur. Therefore when practising a loop drive against a low backspin, a player should not loop a return that is mistakenly placed too high and which could be smashed, because he is being presented a ball to which he should react with a different response. If he starts looping this high ball in practice, the same is likely to happen in a match. Because a loop drive is usually a safer stroke than a smash, many players have concentrated so much on looping that their forehand smash has considerably decreased in efficiency.

Players have to be able to adapt to external factors (visual cues). Examples are the speed of table, the type of floor and the size of the hall.

They must learn to adjust to new conditions. English players who are so used to playing on fast tables are usually very good at counter attacking against each other, but when they go abroad and play on slower tables, their strokes do not propel the ball as fast. Thus the top European players have the time to react and produce a far more effective stroke, like a loop drive, and so be in a better position to dictate play. The way for English players to overcome this is to practise on slower tables, as they are now doing. Before a major championship, the ideal preparation is to practise in identical conditions. The English players now have the ability to play both the 'counter-attacking game' and the 'looping game'.

One should not learn a set of strokes but should learn how to make strokes appropriate to the moment. This is the difference between a habit and a skill at the early stage of learning. Once these skills have been learnt they eventually become habitual. Environment varies little in shot putting, so a habit can be developed, but when the environment is constantly changing, as in table tennis, skill must be applied. When learning table tennis it cannot be overstressed that this is not just a matter of acquiring a series of operations, one by one, and stringing them together. It is always the total organism that does the learning and not just those outer mechanisms that are most conspicuously involved. When playing a stroke, it is not enough to hold the head and body in the right position and to swing the arm in the desired direction if these things are done without reference to each other. It is therefore vital that one develops correct 'motor intentions'.

Table tennis is a game where much attention must be given to the learning of strokes and to the interpretation of spin, speed and direction of the ball from the opponent. Motor skill psychologists define this as an 'open skill' which has to fit either in an unpredictable series of environmental requirements, or in a very exacting series, whether predictable or unpredictable. In open skills like table tennis, a great variety of situations must be met and a player may counter stroke in such a way as to make up for his physical disabilities or bad techniques. Dragutin Surbek of Yugoslavia has been one of the best players in the world for many years, yet his backhand attacking strokes are seldom seen. A table tennis coach must decide whether his players should have a good all round stroke ability or one or two dominating strokes. Stellan Bengtsson of Sweden is a player in the former category while Surbek is more in the latter mould.

Table tennis players need to build up strength, power and endurance to help prevent fatigue when in competition, but one must not overlook the mental fatigue barrier which occurs, especially when playing someone of a higher calibre. Therefore one should realise that the central receptor, translatory and effector mechanisms concerning the organisation of data and the shaping of actions are working extensively in a game of table tennis.* When a player is playing someone below his own standard, there is

* The central receptor mechanism is a part of the body that receives different stimuli from the sensory organs of the body. The translatory mechanism tries to interpret the stimuli and

less mental strain and this allows for longer periods of play without fatigue. Because he has more time to play his strokes, he is not using up the same amount of mental energy. The weaker player is using up much more mental energy because he is trying to think of ways of preventing the better player from dominating the game. The weaker player is also likely to use more physical energy because the better player has more skill in placement and therefore is likely to make the weaker player move more.

Mental fatigue can be eased in practice sessions by not initially making tasks difficult and so limiting the pressures on the central mechanisms. However, one should be careful that over concentration on the effector side does not lower the optimum level of performance.

prepare the best response. The effector mechanism then tries to produce the response.

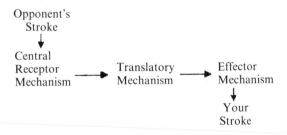

2 Learning to Play Table Tennis

GRIPS AND READY STANCES

Before actually discussing the various strokes and then the progressions to consistency and pressure play I feel it is very important to mention the various grips and ready stances which a player can use and how they can affect the strokes. There are basically two grips – the shake hands grip used mainly in European countries and the penhold grip used mainly in Asia (Figs. 1a–f). Both grips have advantages and disadvantages.

Fig. 1a Shake hands grip **Fig. 1b**

Fig. 1c Penhold grip (Chinese) **Fig. 1d**

Fig. 1e Penhold grip (Japanese) **Fig. 1f**

Penhold grip

There are two main types of penhold grip – the Chinese grip (Figs. 1c and 1d) and the Japanese grip (Figs. 1e and 1f). In the Chinese grip the thumb and index finger are not as close together and the other three fingers are nearer the handle in such a position so that either one, two, or all three of them touch the racket. The advantage of the Chinese grip over the Japanese grip is that more movement is possible in the forearm through the pivot in the arm lever being the radio-ulnar joints* and not the elbow joints. This allows for more power coming from a shorter stroke.

Definitions of strokes vary with the penhold grip. For example, if you talk to a penhold grip player about a backhand push, this is what he calls a 'block'. Also his push is called a 'cut'.

The good point about the penhold grip style is that the position of the racket gives far more scope for flexibility in the wrist when playing forehand strokes or services. This is because the arm extensors and flexors‡ are nearly always free for movement. The penhold players' grip also allows them to manipulate their fingers more easily up and down and around the handle of the racket and so delay the actual spin which they are going to impart on the ball until the very last moment. This timing makes it very difficult for opponents to react quickly for the return. The same reasons apply to the penholder being able to angle the short return of service on the forehand so well. With the shake hands grip wrist extension is limited and so the same range of movements does not exist.

Attacking strokes mainly consist of a type of block or smash. The backhand smash is played when a right-handed player has time to move his left leg back, which makes possible extra stroke preparation and more rotation of the hips and waist to impart more power. The block is played with a more 'square'† stance and often the ball is hit more flatly than by the shake hands grip players. This is because the amount of topspin that can be imparted is minimal in comparison with the backhand loop drive or even topspin of the shake hands grip players. A flat ball can be very difficult for an opponent to return and the penholder's stroke can often cause great difficulty especially if he can angle the ball effectively. The movement from backhand to forehand in a penhold grip is much quicker and this is another reason why this is so effective over the table. Change of stroke can be done by movement of the wrist and radio-ulnar joint, whereas the shake hands grip players have to use the elbow joint more. This longer lever arm increases time in movement.

---

* These joints are included in the capsules of the elbow and wrist joints but if necessary they have separate movements and functions.

‡ Muscles that are primarily responsible for flexion and extension movements of the arm.

† See section on ready stances.

Shake hands grip (Figs. 1a and 1b)

The big advantage which the shake hands grip players have is in their backhand stroke variation, i.e. push, block, counter attack, topspin loop drive, sidespin loop drive and smash. From the mid-fifties up to about 1970 the Asiatics had managed to dominate the Europeans even though Europeans had this advantage. However the Europeans had not developed their strokes to their full potential. Now that they have developed and can loop drive so well with the backhand they can avoid getting out of position so often by attempting a forehand loop drive. This also makes it more difficult for the penhold player to smash the ball. The penhold players do still try to smash the ball but the likelihood of error is greater.*

Because of his more equal strength on both backhand and forehand the shake hands grip player also has the advantage when driven away from the table. He can retrieve quite adequately with both backhand and forehand whereas the penhold player finds it difficult to play a backhand stroke. Therefore the penhold player must try to get onto his forehand side and this requires more movement and the greater chance of getting out of position. A shake hands player, therefore, finds it easier to change his game from 'over the table' to a 'deeper' position if necessary, so as to give himself more time.

Ready stances

Before a player even receives a ball he may well be in danger of losing the point because he is poorly balanced or out of position, so it is very important to consider the ready stance. Certain principles should always be followed. The position of the feet should be marginally wider than the width of the shoulders. Balance should be on the toes so that a small piece of paper could slide under the heels. The knees should be inclined inwards through inversion of the feet (see page 134) and relaxed between flexion and extension to avoid imposing too much tension on the thighs. The stomach muscles should be held firm with the upper body inclined slightly forward and the shoulders be kept slightly in. The shoulders should be comfortable and not stiff or propped upwards. The arms should hang naturally because this is the angle of least fatigue and the elbow should be bent at approximately 90°. Adopt a position that is neither too close nor too far away from the table (Figs. 2a–c).

Attacking players who have strong forehand strokes often take up a ready stance as indicated in Figs. 2a, 2b and 3a. Attacking players who have strong backhand strokes prefer a stance nearer the centre of the table while defensive players take a stance in relation to the centre of the table and with the right foot more forward (Figs. 2c, 3b and 3c). These ready stances give each player the best opportunity of successfully receiving the serve and playing their stronger strokes.

* See Chapter 6 on World Table Tennis.

Fig. 2a

Ready stance

Fig. 2b

Fig. 2c Ready stance (Norbert van de Walle, Belgium)

Fig. 3 (*below*) Ready stances

Key: ● Left foot
× Right foot

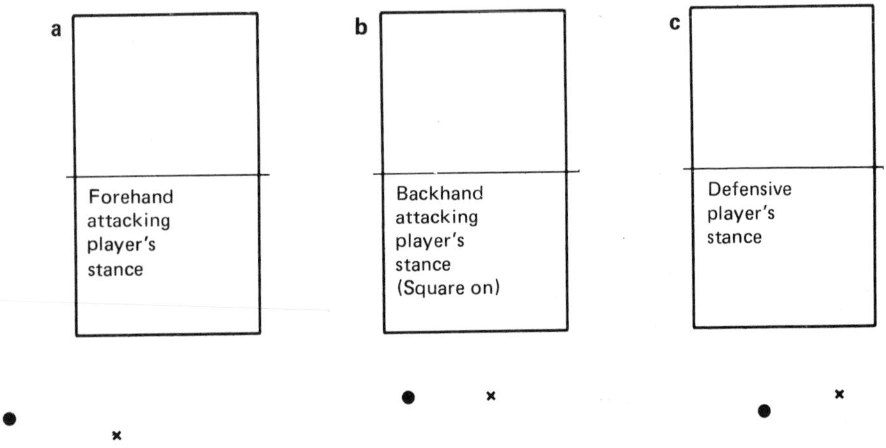

a

Forehand attacking player's stance

b

Backhand attacking player's stance (Square on)

c

Defensive player's stance

● ×

● ×

● ×

MODERN STROKE PLAY

Please note that the strokes are for right-handed players and they are described in set groups, i.e. forehand, backhand, attacking and defensive strokes. They are not necessarily to be taught in this order.

The forehand push (Figs. 4a–d)

This stroke is used mainly as a safety stroke if a player cannot play a more aggressive attacking stroke. It can be played from both the backhand and forehand court and can be very effective in manoeuvring an opponent. In its most effective form it is used when an opponent plays the ball short to your forehand with backspin. With careful manipulation you can play the ball back very short to any part of the table so the opponent cannot obtain a definite opening. A player who possesses good manipulation of the fingers and wrist can often angle the ball in the diagonal direction. If he feels that the opponent is too close to the table then the forehand push can be executed in such a way that the ball travels deep to the baseline. This shot must travel fast and have a good disguised spin on it or the opponent may be able to adjust his balance and perform an attacking stroke which may well be to your detriment. When learning this stroke it is best to play the ball to the middle of the opponent's right hand court and concentrate on playing the stroke with the correct footwork and the following principles.

Fig. 4a

Fig. 4b

Fig. 4c

Fig. 4d

Fig. 5 Right foot leading in returning a short ball. Linda Howard, England (1976 European Ladies Doubles Champion)

NOTE: These principles apply to a ball returned long to the forehand. If the ball is returned short to the forehand the right foot will become the leading foot and not the left foot (Fig. 5).

Notice that when preparing for the stroke there is a transference of the player's body weight onto the right foot and the preliminary stance is such that the right foot is further back in relation to the 'square on' position of a 'ready' stance. One ensures that the body moves correctly so that the racket is moved behind the line of flight of the ball. As one has prepared for the stroke both legs should be flexed, with the left foot pointing generally in the direction in which you want to play the ball and the right foot pointing more towards the continuation of the base line of the table (Fig. 4a).

When coming in to meet the ball the racket will start at approximately chest height with the elbow flexed at about 90° and the racket angle at 'just open'. The more open the racket becomes then the more backspin will be imparted on the ball.

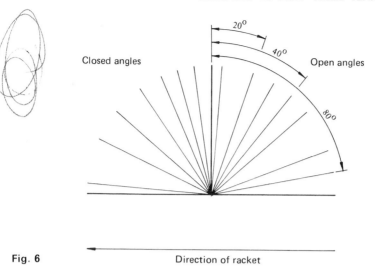

Closed angles

Open angles

20°

40°

80°

Fig. 6   Direction of racket

As the player's body weight is transferred from the right foot to the left foot the racket arm comes in a downward forward direction and contact will be made just in front of the body as the ball is dropping from the peak of its bounce. On contact with the ball there is a rotation in the forearm (supination by the radio-ulnar joint, see page 129), and the ball will travel from the racket in an upward direction. The racket should almost be a continuation of the forearm; otherwise sidespin effects could occur on the ball (Fig. 4b).

This stroke is practised at first when there is little backspin on the ball from the opponent. A gentle guiding action by the use of left spinal rotation is a very important factor which must not be forgotten. It is important to remember not to follow-through too far, especially across the body (Figs. 4c and 4d).

The forehand counter attack (Figs. 7a–d)
This stroke is used against a counter attack or block when neither a smash nor loop drive is possible. The ball travels over the net so fast from the opponent that it is not always possible to find the time to move into a sideways stance, as for the push. One has to improvise by rotating the hips and thorax and pivoting sufficiently with the toes so that the ball is not struck with the racket while the body is too 'square' to the table.

The stroke should start with the weight of the player's body on the right foot. The player should continually watch the ball while rotating the upper body from the right. The elbow is flexed at an angle of approximately 90° and a comfortable distance from the side of the body. The shot is a relatively short movement and contact with the ball is made as it rises or reaches the peak of its bounce (Fig. 7a). Topspin is imparted to the ball as the racket comes behind and over the ball to about chest height. As one

Fig. 7a

approaches the ball the player's body weight is centred mainly on the left foot. The angle of the racket on contact is slightly closed (Fig. 7b). On the follow-through it is essential that the racket does not travel too far across the centre of the body and that it does not finish above the head as this will mean that playing the next stroke will incur the return of the racket over the same distance, and often either this takes too long or one can become off balance (Fig. 7d).

Fig. 7b

Fig. 7c

Fig. 7d

The forehand flick (Figs. 8a–c)

This is an attacking stroke usually used against a service or a push stroke played short over the net. The amount of speed that a player can impart upon the ball will depend upon wrist-joint flexibility, timing and the height of the ball when it is contacted by the racket. Most attacking players rely on the forehand flick to create an 'opening' for them to follow up with a more forceful attacking stroke. The ability of the player to be deceptive in the placement of the ball is often more important than the speed of the ball, in enabling him to prevent the opponent from moving to play an aggressive attacking stroke. Ideally, a player should try to obtain a good combination of deception, angle of trajectory and speed when playing a forehand flick.

When playing against a sidespin or sidespin topspin service placed to the

Fig. 8a   Fig. 8b   Fig. 8c

forehand or the middle of the table, the right arm movements are very similar to a counter attacking stroke (Fig. 7). However, when playing against a 'short' ball, the footwork is similar to that of a forehand push against a ball that has been pushed just over the net (Fig. 4).

When receiving a push or backspin service, the racket angle will be closed and the precise angle will depend upon the amount of backspin on the ball. The contact point between the racket and the ball should be on the upper hemisphere of the ball and at the peak of the bounce. The racket moves mainly in a forward plane and slightly in an upward plane. If there is only a little backspin on the ball and it bounces 'short', but high, it may be possible to move the racket downwards towards the ball.

For the forehand flick to a short returned ball, a player should concentrate on positioning the right leg well under the table, which will necessitate a flexing of the right knee joint. The right foot should be pointing in the direction of where the ball will be approximately contacted. The left leg should not be over-extended or leave the ground; otherwise the body will be improperly balanced. If the left foot is positioned too far away from the right foot, the player will also find it difficult to move quickly into position for his next stroke (Fig. 8a).

When preparing to play the forehand flick, the player must anticipate the direction of the ball and where it is going to reach the peak of its bounce. He must then move his body so that his racket is positioned approximately one foot behind the expected peak of the bounce and in line with the flight of the ball. As the racket moves forward to make contact with the ball, the upper body should be inclined forward over the right leg and the right arm extended at approximately 165° at the elbow (Fig. 8b). The direction of the ball from the forehand flick can be altered at the last moment by varying the amount of flexion or extension in the wrist joint. The left arm is positioned away from the left side of the body so as to assist in balance during the stroke. The stroke should have a short follow-through so the player may move quickly away from the table for his next stroke (Fig. 8c).

Fig. 9a   Fig. 9b   Fig. 9c

The forehand smash (Figs. 9a–c)

The forehand smash is usually played when a ball has been placed at a position on the table at a certain height so that you can attempt a shot which will not be returned by the opposition. It is normally very powerful and accuracy will only come with constant practice. Every player usually has a slight variation in the action of a forehand smash but certain principles must apply. It is necessary for a player to position himself so that he is going to make contact with the ball at the peak of its bounce or as it ascends or descends to shoulder height. If contact is made before these points there is a greater element of risk involved in the stroke.

To get in the preliminary position for a forehand smash, much will depend on where the peak of the bounce occurs. It is important that one gets the racket behind the ball in such a way that one is not off balance or stretching. For every forehand smash, one should position the body so that the angle of the racket is closed upon contact with the ball. This means that the main variable will be the movement of the feet over different distances to ensure the stroke remains similar. Sometimes it may only be necessary to pivot on the toes of one foot while moving the other foot.

From the ready stance position one would move the right foot, then the left foot, almost simultaneously, so that the body is at a more side-on position to the table. The left arm is moved forward to balance the body as the right arm draws back to commence the stroke (Fig. 9a). The arm swing will vary according to where the height of the bounce will be, or if it is too high, then at shoulder height. The contact point will also affect the amount that the racket is 'closed'. When making contact with the ball it is essential that the body is moving forwards. The player's body weight should be on the toes of a flexed left leg during contact with the ball and as the follow-through occurs the degree of extension in the knee joint of the right leg should increase as flexion increases in the knee joint of the left leg, but the right foot should try and remain in contact with the ground.

The player should watch the ball very carefully and the head and trunk of the body should move as one part. To ensure that the ball travels over the net correctly the follow-through should be in the direction of the ball. Only after completing the follow-through should one change the feet and body position in preparation for the next stroke (Fig. 9c).

The forehand topspin loop drive (Figs. 10a–e)

This is one of the most useful strokes in table tennis but it is difficult to learn. There are many variations because it is a stroke which can be used against a ball that has been pushed, chopped*, counter attacked, blocked or looped. It should be a means of setting up the ball for a forehand smash if an outright winner cannot be achieved. Because so much topspin is placed on the ball it is very difficult for someone defending to keep the ball low over the net continually. More physical energy is used in performing this stroke than any other because there is a greater range of movement in all parts of the body and the speed of the racket on contact with the ball can be very fast.

As with the forehand smash it is important to try and get to a reasonable sideways stance and a wide base so that correct balance is kept throughout the stroke. The knees are flexed, more so than for any other forehand shot, so that the arm can draw the racket nearer the floor and the stroke will be longer and on contact with the ball the racket will have travelled further and gained more momentum. On commencing the stroke the player's body weight should be distributed mainly on the right foot and the right elbow should be extended to almost 180° while the left arm maintains body balance by being forward and flexed at the elbow (Fig. 10b).

As the racket travels up to meet the ball at the side or just in front of the body the racket arm becomes more flexed at the elbow, the knee joints extend, and the player's body weight is transferred onto the left foot while the toes of the right foot can remain in contact with the ground or the momentum of the rotation of the body can move it forward. Whether or not the rear foot is moving, there is a definite rotation of the hips and thorax so that the upper part of the body finishes in more of a square-on position to the table. The angle and height of the bounce at which the racket contacts the ball will depend upon the amount of backspin or topspin imparted by the opponent.

---

* 'Chopped' – *i.e.* played with backspin.

Fig. 10a   Fig. 10b

Fig. 10c   Fig. 10d

If playing topspin so that the ball is contacted as in 'A' (Fig. 11), the point of contact will be preferably just after the peak of the bounce. The stroke will eventually produce medium spin and speed and is very useful against light backspin, counter attack, pushes or blocked returns.

If playing a topspin so that the ball is contacted as in 'B', the stroke is usually played at a time when the ball is descending. This stroke produces more of a lifting effect on the ball and is very useful against heavy backspin or push.

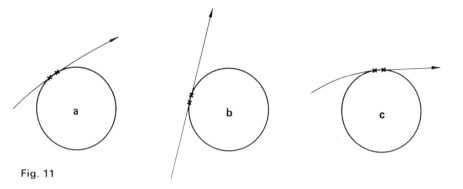

Fig. 11

If playing a topspin so that the ball is contacted as in 'C' one has to have a high degree of co-ordination and skill. This contact point produces a fast speed plus spin and the contact point is at the peak of the bounce. The stroke can be effective against a light push, counter attack block or loop drive. The idea is for a vicious brushing effect to take place as the racket moves upwards and forwards. As with the other looping strokes the follow-through and racket deceleration should result in the racket coming above the head. From this position the whole body should return to the ready position for the next stroke (Fig. 10d and Fig. 12).

Fig. 12 Forehand topspin loop drive, by Jacques Secretin, France (1976 European Men's Singles Champion and 1977 World Mixed Doubles Champion)

Fig. 13a

Fig. 13b

Fig. 13c

Fig. 13d

The forehand topspin sidespin loop drive (Fig. 13a–d)
At one stage in the history of the game it became quite
easy for a 'blocker' to return a loop because nearly
everyone had the same kind of spin on the ball. So it
was found necessary to develop a stroke which looked
similar, but had a different spin variation, so that if the
blocker attempted the normal stroke to counteract the
topspin loop, he would lose the point. Like the topspin
loop, the topspin sidespin loop can be used against
almost every shot produced by an opponent, but in the
early stages of learning it is best used against a push or
light backspin.

The position of the feet, left arm and racket are very
similar at the beginning of the stroke to the topspin loop
but the actual racket movement will be different. The
arm is kept straighter and, on contact with the ball,
slightly in front of the body, the racket travels round its outside by a flexion
of the wrist joint. The racket actually makes an arc shape from near the
right knee out towards the right side of the table before coming in towards
the centre of the body in the direction of the net (Figs. 13a and 13b). The
body and right arm are moving as one during the rotational arc and the
player's body weight is transferred onto the left foot. On the follow-
through, the racket could cross the face as a result of the momentum built
up during the stroke (Figs. 13c and 13d). To achieve the correct stroke,
the wrist is positioned so that the ball makes contact at the same point on
the racket as the topspin loop but the top of the racket is facing more
towards the ground instead of the side.

The forehand block (Figs. 14a–d)
This has been a very important stroke especially since the introduction of
the loop drive in the early 1960s. It is a good answer to the various types of

Fig. 14a

Fig. 14b

Fig. 14c

Fig. 14d

spin imparted by the loop and it is now being proved that the once deadly loop drive is not so advantageous if someone masters its return. Depending on the amount of topspin and sidespin imparted by the loop, a player merely alters the angle of his racket on the block stroke to return the ball safely. Basically one judges where the ball will bounce, its direction after bouncing and the type of spin employed, and then it is a question of moving the feet to a position similar to that of the forehand push so that the racket is directly behind the ball, facing sideways and slightly upwards (Fig. 14a). An exception to this general rule is if the ball bounces short to the forehand. In this instance the right foot moves forwards to become the leading foot when contact is made with the ball. If the ball is blocked with the forehand in front of the body then the racket will be pointing more upwards in a closed angle (Fig. 14d).

The stroke depends entirely on touch and it is essential that everything is done with perfect timing. The racket should be very lightly held and on the approach the whole body should be moving slightly upwards and forwards by means of a slight raising of the body by the toes. As contact is made with the ball when it is rising, there should be hardly any forceful movement of the racket and it should act like a cushion when the ball hits it. On contact, the arm raises the racket slightly forwards and so has a guiding effect on the ball, so that the topspin produced by the loop drive carries the ball back to the opponent. How well one can foresee how much spin is on the ball from a loop drive will determine one's success in countering it because the angle of the racket on the block will have to alter accordingly. This can only come with experience but if one remembers the cushioning effect then success should eventually occur. One must also remember that the heavier the topspin then the more the racket is 'closed' (Figs. 14b and 14c).

Fig. 15a

The forehand drop shot (Fig. 15a–c)

In modern table tennis this stroke is not used very often because when two attacking players face each other, the opportunities of performing a drop shot rarely occur. The forehand drop shot is used when the opponent has been forced away from the table and is made to play a defensive backspin stroke to the opponent's forehand court. The ball will return just over the net and usually the attacking player can either smash the ball or play the drop shot. Most top players prefer to attempt the winning smash because they have all 'angles' of the table to aim at, but if they have been missing their forehand smashes they may find it safer to play the drop shot. If performed correctly, this should give the opponent little opportunity to return the ball, and if he does, it will be a scrambled effort so that he sets the ball up for the attacker to play a winning shot on the next stroke. It is more difficult for a player to perform a drop shot from a ball near to his own baseline as the ball may 'sit up' so that the defender can move in and hit the return. The whole concept of the drop shot is to guide the ball just over the net into the opponent's court, so that if he left it, it would bounce at least twice before going off the table (Fig. 16). It is therefore a sound theory that the nearer the ball is to the baseline then the more difficult it is to play the shot, because the distance the ball has to travel is further and the height of the parabola is greater so as to allow for net clearance. The increased height and length will tend to make the ball bounce more, and so there is a likelihood of it 'sitting up' or travelling off the end of the table so as to make it easier for the successful return.

When playing a forehand drop shot off the short return the following principles apply. The oncoming ball will be in a position to smash; otherwise the drop shot would be called a push. The ball therefore travels high over the net from the defender and bounces up high from the table. The attacker sees the opponent a long way from the table and in a good

Fig. 15b

Fig. 15c

position to return a smash. The attacker perceives that he is going to smash the ball but at the last moment will change his stroke to the drop shot (Figs. 15a and 15b). In the preliminary stages one is in the final position to smash

Fig. 16

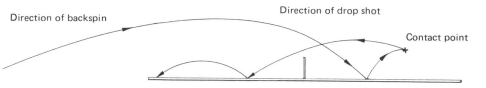

Direction of backspin

Direction of drop shot

Contact point

the ball with the racket coming down to make contact and the player's body weight mainly on the front foot. As the ball reaches the top of its bounce one suddenly checks the stroke and rotates the forearm of the flexed right arm so that the hand travels from a pronated to supinated position (see page 129). This involves the racket travelling through an arc of about 85° and changing from a closed position to a very open one. Instead of coming

Fig. 17

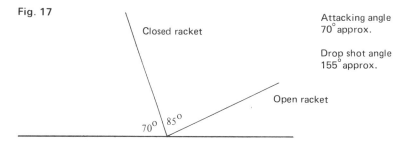

Closed racket

Attacking angle 70° approx.

Drop shot angle 155° approx.

Open racket

70° 85°

Fig. 18a

down on the ball with a closed racket one will travel up to meet it with an open racket. During this time the player's body weight is being redistributed to both feet, though both legs are flexed at the knee joints, the left slightly more than the right. All that is required now, is for the attacker to move the racket slightly forward and up by a flexing movement of the shoulder joint. The impact should be very slight and only give enough momentum to the ball for it to drop over the net. The important things to remember are a 'loose grip' so one can obtain a cushioning effect on the ball and for the player's body weight to end up on the front left foot. There is little follow-through of the arm, or the ball will be made to travel too far and so ruin the effect of the stroke (Fig. 15c).

The backhand push (Figs. 18a–c)
In top level table tennis this stroke is used less and less as the increased fitness of players enables them to get into position where they can play more attacking strokes like the backhand and forehand loop drives. However, it still serves as an important part of the game, especially if the ball is played really short with backspin on the backhand side, or if one's recovery from a previous stroke is a little too slow for an effective attacking stroke to be made. As in the forehand push, a flexible wrist and good arm mobility will greatly assist in placement that will not be detrimental to you. Once again you should try to angle the ball short or play the ball long if your opponent is cramped over the table.

The execution of the stroke is best learnt in the beginning stages by using a 'side stance' where the left foot is behind and to the outside of the right foot. If one wishes to dominate with forehand strokes the feet will be positioned in more of a 'square on' stance or with the right foot slightly behind the line of the left in relation to the edge of the table. It may not be

Fig. 18b

Fig. 18c

possible to move the feet into the correct position in a quick rally so one must always improvise upon the two stances.

On preparing for the stroke the racket is brought back to the chest or slightly to the left of the chest and this movement is associated with the player transferring the body weight so that movement into the ball can use all the available guidance of the whole body. The elbow is once again at about 90° on commencement of the stroke and the racket angle is open. As the racket comes forward and downward to meet the ball, the elbow is extending, the shoulder is flexing and abducting (see page 129), and the weight is being transferred to the front foot while the racket will come under the descending ball so that this time the forearm rotates towards a pronated position. The racket is again a continuation of the forearm and the follow-through should stop just before the forearm straightens or the racket travels too far across the body.

The backhand counter attack (Figs. 19a–d)

This stroke is often used in table tennis and it is usual for an 'attacker' to have a very consistent backhand counter attack if he is to be a successful player. The objective behind the stroke is to keep the ball under control and then place the ball in a position so that one can follow-up with a winning stroke like a forehand loop drive or smash. In a game between two attacking players who do not have outstanding loop drives it is inevitable that many of each player's strokes will be the backhand counter attack, but it is interesting to note that against a defensive player it is very unlikely that the attacker will ever play this shot as it is not effective against backspin.

The player's body should be positioned behind the line of the oncoming ball so that if a stroke was not played the ball would make contact with the left side of the body. The left foot should be slightly in front of the right foot

Fig. 19a

in relation to the line of the ball and the body should be balanced on the toes while the knees are flexed in a 'jockey's' position. The stomach muscles should be held firm, the chest pushed out and the eyes should be focussed towards the white line at the opponent's end of the table. The left arm should be flexed at the elbow at approximately the same angle as the racket arm, as this will help in maintaining balance. The stroke starts from the waistline area of the body with the hand kept below the line of the elbow. Contact with the ball should be made at the earliest opportunity above net height, preferably over the table. When contact is made with the ball, the racket face is slightly closed and it is coming forward and upward to impart topspin. At this stage the arm will be in such a position that the hand and the elbow will be nearly parallel to the surface of the table. The follow-through should not be too long and should not come too far across the body; otherwise one may lose balance and fail to change position quickly enough for the next shot (Fig. 19d).

After considerable practice this stroke should be working like a piston and it is possible not to take the eyes off the far edge of the table because one should be able to develop an insight into where the ball is going to bounce. This does not apply if the ball travels to a position where another type of stroke will be necessary. The focussing of the eyes on the edge of the table instead of on the ball has two distinct advantages. Firstly, it allows one to keep a constant watch on the position of the opponent so one can be prepared to play a backhand quickly to a place beyond his reach. Secondly, this helps the player to see what type of stroke his opponent is likely to play and in what direction. If one jerks the head every time one plays a backhand counter attack this positioning sense becomes more difficult.

The backhand flick (Fig. 20a–c)
If the mechanical principles of the previous strokes have been understood, there is little need to explain in depth the mechanics of the backhand flick,

Fig. 19b	Fig. 19c	Fig. 19d

as they include certain principles of the other strokes.

When a push or service from the opponent is placed to the backhand court of the table, then the backhand flick can be used. It is used for the same reasons as the forehand flick and the racket is at a closed angle, the degree of which will depend upon the spin of the oncoming ball. The approach of the racket to the ball is similar to the backhand counter attack when returning a sidespin topspin service, and to a forehand flick when returning a backspin sidespin stroke, except that the right leg is placed forward, under the table, to assist in the balance of the body during the execution of the stroke.

Fig. 20a	Fig. 20b	Fig. 20c

Fig. 21a   Fig. 21b

The backhand smash (Figs. 21a–d)
This stroke is best used when the ball is reasonably high in the backhand
court and either there is not enough time or one is in too bad a position to
move around and play the forehand smash. In modern table tennis when
two attacking players play each other the ball is travelling too fast to play a
backhand smash off a normal counter attack because there is insufficient
time to place the feet and the racket in the correct position for the preparation of the stroke. Against the defensive player who is backspinning
the ball, the backhand smash is usually a risky shot, especially as a
forehand smash is dominant in the majority of players, and it is easier to
teach the correct footwork to a player so he can move around to the
backhand to play his forehand. Usually there is ample time to get into this
forehand position because the ball is travelling a longer distance and at a
slower speed than from an attacking opponent.

With the backhand smash it is important at first to get the body into a
side-stance position. This is done by a small movement of the feet so that
the right part of the hip slightly faces the table, with the right foot more
forward than the left, and at such a distance that the ball can be struck at
one of its highest points after the bounce. At the commencement of the
stroke the weight of the player's body should be slightly on the toes of the
back foot, but both feet should be firmly on the ground. The knees should
be slightly flexed and the left foot should be nearly parallel with the end of
the table; the right foot faces in the direction of the intended line of play.

The racket commences at about hip height and as it is brought forward to
make contact with the ball, body weight is being transferred towards the
front foot and as the thorax becomes more 'square' to the table the racket
rises to just below chest height. The arm is beginning to straighten and the

Fig. 21c

Fig. 21d

wrist is rotating so that the racket is coming over as well as forwards on the ball and imparting slight topspin. During the stroke the left arm is flexed at about 120° so as to assist balance (Fig. 21c). The ball should travel very fast and straight, so on the follow-through there should be more forward movement than upward movement. There should always be a closed angle of the racket on contact with the ball. After the follow-through the stroke should be decelerated quickly and then brought back to a ready position for the next stroke (Fig. 21d).

The backhand topspin loop drive (Fig. 22a–c)
This is one of the most difficult strokes in table tennis. It is a very effective stroke for lifting heavy backspin services or strokes. A player who has not reached an advanced stage in table tennis would normally be happy to push the ball but this would be fatal because it gives the attacking initiative to the other player by enabling him to loop drive the long backspin return. There are numerous variations of backhand loop drives used on the Continent since many national coaches develop different styles of attacking players. There are general principles which are common to all strokes.

The ball is contacted just in front or to the left side of the body and although the positioning of the feet is almost the same as a ready stance (Fig. 3b), the knee flexion is greater at the commencement of the stroke. The left arm assists in balance as in previous strokes, the chest and stomach muscles are held firm, but this time the racket starts from a lower position through the arm being more extended (Fig. 22a). As the legs extend at the knee joint there is a quick movement of the forearm so the racket is travelling very fast in an almost vertical plane. Just before contact is made with the ball, there is a quick wrist abduction action which further increases

Fig. 22a (*above*)

Fig. 22c (*below*)

Fig. 22b

the speed of the racket. During contact the racket moves slightly forward but the main emphasis is an upward movement so tremendous topspin is imparted and the ball travels across the net in an arc shape (Figs. 22b and 22c). The arc will become shallower if more forward emphasis is placed on the stroke. Plenty of follow-through is necessary to allow the contact between ball and racket to be as long as possible.

The best contact point will depend upon the stroke used by the opponent, and it should be similar to the contact point chosen when performing a forehand topspin loop drive.

The backhand block (Figs. 23a–d)

This shot can be used against the smash of an opponent but its accuracy involves an element of luck as the ball is travelling very fast when contact is made. One must hope that a reflex action will assist in placing the racket in the correct blocking position. As with the forehand block it is mainly used against an attacker who specialises in the loop drive.

The feet, body and arm positions are the same as at the start of the counter attack. As the ball is travelling towards a player he must judge the amount of topspin and sidespin upon it. He must then move the racket in line with the forearm and parallel to the near edge of the table. If the ball travels fast and high to the line of the body then it may be necessary to play a stroke vertically above the elbow so the racket is pointing towards the ceiling. As in the forehand block, touch and timing are vital (Fig. 23d). The racket is held lightly and on the approach to contact, the whole body should be moving slightly upwards and forwards by means of a gentle rising on the toes. The correct angle of the racket to cushion the ball will only come with experience but the general principle is that as contact is made the racket is brought slightly forward and upwards. The more topspin imparted then the more closed the racket face becomes. To counter sidespin, wrist movements are needed to make sure the racket face meets the direction of the ball at the correct angle. Little follow-through is necessary and so positioning for the next shot is quite easy.

Fig. 23a

Fig. 23b

Fig. 23d

Fig. 23c

Fig. 24a

The backhand drop shot (Figs. 24a–c)
Few players use a backhand smash because they often find it easier to move around to the backhand court to play a forehand smash. Because a backhand smash is infrequently used it follows that a backhand drop shot should rarely be played. If an opponent is forced to play a backspin stroke and he plays the ball reasonably high and short to the backhand court of the table he can usually react more quickly to a possible drop shot because he can notice that the attacker is not moving around to play the forehand and he knows that there is generally a reluctance for players to attempt a backhand smash.

In the preliminary stages of the stroke the racket and body are in the backhand smash position. As the ball reaches the top of its bounce, the racket moving towards the ball alters its angle of approach as in the forehand drop shot. There is flexion in both knee joints and on contact with the ball there is a gentle rising on the toes, a slight extending of the knee joints and the right arm moves forwards. A 'cushioning effect' should result if one grips the racket loosely enough and the amount of forward and upward movement of the racket should just be sufficient to carry the ball over the net. There is little follow-through with the right arm, and the left arm, as in all other strokes, acts as an assistance to balance throughout.

The forehand backspin (Figs. 25a–d)
As in the case of the simple pushing action on the backhand and forehand, the forehand backspin tends to be the more difficult stroke to master, especially the balancing of the body and the control of the follow-through during the stroke. It is usually used to counteract a loop drive or smash which has been placed in the right hand court of the table. The player should get behind the line of the ball and direct it in a line of flight which

Fig. 24b

Fig. 24c

allows the maximum opportunity for the returning ball to hit the opponent's court, i.e. a diagonal direction. In more advanced play the defensive player should try to place the ball in the most awkward position for the attacking player to play a forceful stroke. The action of the stroke will vary according to the speed and spin already on the ball, but always the defensive player's aim should be to create the opportunity either to float the ball or backspin it heavily.

Let us first examine the action of a forehand defensive stroke which imparts quite an amount of backspin and then mention how one can disguise the amount of backspin. Against a topspin loop drive a player should judge the direction of the ball, and then move away and sideways to the end of the table so as to allow much of the speed and spin to be lost off the ball and preferably to make contact just above waist height as the ball is descending. The feet should be far enough apart to give a good balanced position. The left foot should be facing the direction in which the player wants the ball to travel while the right foot should be behind and to the right of the upper body with the toes pointing out to the side. The weight of the player's body should be on the back foot with flexion in the knee joint. The left foot should remain in contact with the ground and there should be a little flexion in the knee joint of the left leg. The racket should be held at about shoulder height with the arm flexed at the elbow, about six inches from the side of the body (Fig. 25a). Stretching should be avoided if possible, and all strokes should have a similar preliminary stage. The racket should not be held tightly and should be at an open angle of about 50° (Fig. 26a). The eyes are kept continually on the ball and as one approaches to make contact with the ball the player's body weight is transferred from the back foot towards the front foot so that the centre of gravity of the body is more central and both legs are more or less equally flexed at the knee joint. Body

Fig. 25a   Fig. 25b

weight is on the big toe of the right rear foot and all toes of the left foot. As one comes to this position the racket is travelling towards the ball at an angle to counteract the spin. Contact should be made just above the waist at the side of the body with the elbow a few inches from the mid-abdomen area and flexed at approximately 90° (Fig. 25b).

The racket cuts under the ball to impart backspin; the longer contact can be made with the ball and the faster the racket can meet the ball, the greater will be the backspin produced. Extra speed of approach can be created by faster adduction of the wrist joint as one is just about to make contact with the ball. After the follow-through the racket will travel below waist height and body weight be transferred to the front left foot, with the flexion in the knee joint being more marked than in the rear leg which has almost fully extended. It is essential that the follow-through does not result in the racket cutting too far across the mid-line of the body. Throughout the stroke the left arm assists in balancing the body (Figs. 25c and 25d).

One must adjust the stroke to meet varying amounts of topspin. If one wishes continually to impart a considerable amount of backspin on the ball one must make sure that if the opponent has put more topspin on the ball, then the angle of the racket should be less open and the descent to the ball more vertical, or more open and the descent to the ball more horizontal (Figs. 26a–d). If a player is really skilful he can use a vertical backspin stroke to a ball which is still rising or has reached the top of its bounce. If one wishes to disguise the amount of backspin on the ball and actually not put much backspin on the ball, i.e. Float, the action is quite simple and can easily deceive the opponent. The speed of the racket is slowed up and on meeting the ball the racket moves more in a horizontal plane than a vertical plane or suddenly stops in its downward track (Fig. 26d).

Fig. 25c

Fig. 25d

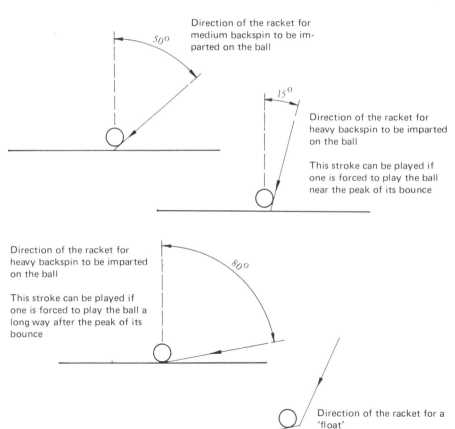

Direction of the racket for medium backspin to be imparted on the ball

50°

Direction of the racket for heavy backspin to be imparted on the ball

This stroke can be played if one is forced to play the ball near the peak of its bounce

15°

Direction of the racket for heavy backspin to be imparted on the ball

This stroke can be played if one is forced to play the ball a long way after the peak of its bounce

80°

Direction of the racket for a 'float'

Fig. 26

The forehand topspin lob (Figs. 27a–e)

This can be a very effective stroke but it is of vital importance that the stroke is administered correctly or the point is likely to be won by the opponent. It is used mainly against a smash or occasionally against a loop drive. A defensive player will usually try to backspin the ball but if he is out of position and stretching, he may find it more beneficial to play the topspin lob. An attacking player often prefers to lob the ball if caught in a defensive position because it sometimes offers more opportunity of getting into an attacking rhythm again and so avoids the possibility of getting permanently 'pinned down' to his weaker defensive strokes.

Some attacking players can be exceptionally good against the heavy backspin defensive players because of their excellent loop drives. It is quite noticeable, however, that many top players who have good loop drives have spent so much time perfecting this stroke that they have tended to neglect practising the forehand smash. Consequently, if a defensive player can perfect the topspin lob this really leaves his opponent no alternative but to try and smash the ball, which could well force him into errors. The ideal topspin lob should have plenty of height and topspin and land within six inches of the opponent's end of the table and so as to make him move to the backhand court to attempt a forehand smash. He cannot risk the difficult backhand smash, and he needs to wait for the spin to be reduced to eliminate the chance of error. However, as he retreats from the table, the defensive player has the opportunity of getting into a good position for the next stroke. The alternative to smashing the lob is to block it, but this often gives advantage to the defensive player because he has limited the force and spin imparted by the attacking player.

The stroke is played when one is well away from the table and in the preliminary stages one can be in a more 'square' stance to the table than the position for the forehand backspin. The left foot will be pointing towards the table while the right foot is behind and to the right side. The player's body weight is mainly on the toes of the right foot and both the knees are slightly flexed. The racket should be below waist height and the racket arm's elbow joint should be at about 140° and not too far from the body (Fig. 27a). The ball should be contacted as it is descending and the player's weight is evenly distributed to both feet and the racket is moving upwards.

Fig. 27b

Fig. 27c

Fig. 27d

Fig. 27e

As one extends the knee joints the racket is brought up at an open angle to make contact with the ball, so that the correct topspin and height of trajectory are obtained. Usually this contact is at about chest height (Fig. 27c). The angle and direction of the racket on contact are vitally important. The angle of the racket and the speed of contact will affect the amount of spin on the ball, while the direction will affect the curvature of the parabola. The essential thing is to obtain a compromise so that with the racket sufficiently under the ball but coming up behind it to create lift, fineness of touch and control of speed will produce enough spin. On the completion of the stroke, the player's body weight should be on the front foot and the racket should be at about head height but not obscuring the vision.

The forehand topspin sidespin lob (Figs. 28a–d)

This stroke has a similar effect to the topspin lob in terms of effectiveness against the attacking player. The additional problem it presents to the opponent is that he has to cope with a certain sideways movement as well as forward and upward movement of the ball off the table. It is used in the same instances as the topspin lob but it is performed slightly differently so

Fig. 28a

Fig. 28b

as to provide the ball with a different path of flight. Really it is almost a defensive stroke becoming an attacking stroke because if administered correctly it can force the attacking player to play a safety shot and so lose the forcing initiative.

As with the topspin lob it should only be used when the ball comes on the forehand side of the table. If one attempts to play a forehand stroke on the backhand side, the whole of the forehand court is 'left open' and this area will often be monopolised by the opponent with the next stroke. If any lob drops short of the baseline by more than a foot then a reasonable attacking player can make the defensive player pay dearly for his mistake.

The footwork in the preliminary stages is the same as in the topspin lob but there is a difference in the arm action which causes a different angle of approach to the ball. The racket is held below waist height, while the body weight is on the back foot as in the topspin lob. As the body is moved towards a more forward position the balance is distributed equally on both feet. The racket moves upwards as if to make contact underneath the ball but then the wrist is flexed so that the racket can contact the outside of the ball (Figs. 28a and 28b). The contact point occurs with an open racket between waist and chest height at about one foot from the body, as the ball is descending, but by the time the ball leaves the racket the racket should be further up and away from the body. A rotation to the left by the thorax will assist in the arc movement of the right arm, which will affect the amount of spin that is put on the ball and also influence the follow-through. The player's racket should not pass too far across the centre of the body and the weight of his body should be on the left foot at the end of the stroke. By the completion of the stroke (including the follow-through) the position of the player's body should be square to the direction of the ball.

Fig. 28c

Fig. 28d

The backhand backspin (Figs. 29a–d)

This is nearly always the defensive player's most used stroke against his attacking opponent. The reason for this is that most players are right handed and the most ineffective stroke of an attacker against the defender is the backhand topspin. Most defensive players therefore play down the backhand side of their opponent and this necessitates the frequent use of the backhand backspin. Once the attacking player moves around to play the more effective forehand strokes, the defensive player can then start changing the direction of his backhand backspin to force the attacker into errors connected with moving and positioning for a stroke. The position of the body and angle of the racket on contact with the ball can be influenced by the speed and spin imparted by the opponent. The action of the strokes against a loop drive that is not too excessive can be as follows:

As the ball is approaching one should judge the direction and make sure that the feet are positioned so that the racket is behind the line of flight. In the preliminary stages the weight of the player's body should be on the back foot, which should point in a line reasonably parallel to the end of the table, while the right foot should point towards the table. The left knee should be flexed while the right leg is reasonably straight (Fig. 29a). The eyes should be kept on the ball and the racket arm flexed so that the racket is positioned near the left of the left shoulder. When approaching the ball the player's body weight becomes evenly distributed on both feet and the racket comes down in an angle of declination so that it will cut under the ball. During the contact with the ball the player's body weight is transferred to the front foot so that the right leg becomes more flexed at the knee joint and the left leg extends (Figs. 29b and 29c). The racket meets the ball at an open angle of about 40° to the horizontal and if extra spin is necessary one can use a quick abduction action of the wrist to create extra speed of movement of the

Fig. 29a   Fig. 29b

Fig. 29c   Fig. 29d

racket. As explained during the forehand backspin, extra spin can be obtained by moving down or under the ball at a greater angle or by increasing the speed of approach.

When applying heavy backspin by coming down viciously on the ball the stroke will necessitate the follow-through of the racket to below the waist but not as far in front of it as with the previously described stroke. This is a more difficult stroke to perfect. However, it is very important to learn because it may be required against a severe loop drive if one wishes to play the ball near the peak of the bounce. During all these strokes it is essential to try and have a sideways stance and never to bring the racket too far across the body, otherwise balance will be severely affected. There is,

however, an exception; it is usually in the 'float ball' stroke that it occurs.
When a ball is looped or smashed to the body it is usually easier to get into a satisfactory position with the backhand defence than with the forehand defence. One often does not have time to move the feet into the correct position for the backhand stroke and so one is committed to have the whole body behind the line of flight of the ball. In this case one must abandon the preliminary stage, when the racket should be about six inches outside the left shoulder, at shoulder height. When one is caught in this 'square position' it is best to have the same degree of flexion in both knee joints and have the heels just off the ground. The racket should start its descent just below chin height and travel with an open angle of about 20° to the vertical line to meet the ball. The final angle will depend upon how much topspin one has judged to be on the ball. During the follow-through the racket will suddenly stop its downward projection and move in a horizontal direction towards the table by an extension of the elbow joint.

The 'floated ball' has little spin and if the stroke is administered correctly it can create difficulties for the attacker because he will have to play a completely different stroke in order to ensure that his next stroke does not send the ball off the end of the table. The float backspin can be used in any position but when the ball is not straight at the body one can position the feet correctly as in the backhand heavy backspin, and the preliminary stages will be similar, although the contact and follow-through are different and prescribed as above.

The backhand topspin lob (Figs. 30a–d)
Like the forehand topspin lob this can be a very effective stroke but it must have the correct height and length in the parabola it describes in order to make it bounce near the opponent's end of the table; otherwise it will most probably be smashed by the opponent. It is used in similar circumstances to the forehand topspin lob both by attacking and defensive players, except that the ball is on the backhand side of the table. When the ball is coming fast towards the body and one cannot move into the correct position, the backhand lob is preferred to the forehand lob. The position of the feet is similar to the backhand backspin.

One should not be overstretching for the shot or be off balance, and at the commencement of the stroke the knees should be flexed and the racket positioned below waist height on the left side of the body (Fig. 30a). On contact at the side and in front of the body, the legs should begin to straighten and the racket should come up and over the ball after the initial stage where it is behind and below the ball (Fig. 30b). The speed and fineness of touch will determine the amount of topspin that will be imparted to the ball. On completion of the stroke one should remain balanced with the racket extended in the air at about head height but one should avoid losing sight of the ball.

Fig. 30a

Fig. 30b

Fig. 30c

Fig. 30d

The backhand topspin sidespin lob (Figs. 31a–d)
Like the topspin lob this can be a very important stroke if performed correctly and it can convert a defensive game into an attacking game if used at an opportune time. However, it is unlikely to be used by a purely defensive player unless he is in a desperate situation and cannot play a sound backspin stroke or because the attacker can play better against backspin than sidespin. It is used under the same circumstances as the forehand topspin sidespin lob except that the ball will be on the backhand side of the table. It is also one of the most difficult strokes to play for a defensive player or for an attacker forced into a defensive position, and only a few players in England really use it effectively. As with most lobbing strokes one must have very good footwork to move into the correct position; otherwise the ball will not gain the necessary spin, speed and length to prevent the opponent making a winning smash.

In the preliminary stages of the stroke the feet should be in a position similar to the topspin lob but the racket should be positioned approximately below waist height and nearer the centre of the body so that one has plenty of opportunity to create a sidespin as well as topspin

Fig. 31a

Fig. 31b

Fig. 31c

Fig. 31d

movement. On contact with the ball one should rise on the toes and through the shoulder and the elbow joint the right arm should bring the racket forward and upwards to meet the ball with an open face at about one foot from the body (Figs. 31a and 31b). This time the racket comes from behind and below the ball, then makes contact around the left side so as to impart topspin and sidespin. Once again there has been a wrist action producing movement from a pronated to a more supinated position. On completion of the stroke the weight of the body should be more on the front foot and the racket should not obscure the player's vision (Fig. 31d).

3 Service and the Return of Service

THE SERVICE

Aims of the service

Many people consider the service as a stroke which starts off the rally and only introduces the ball into play. This theory of the service was evident in the decades when pimpled rubber rackets were mainly used but with the introduction of new rubber and sponge, tremendous spin can be imparted upon the ball and the service is now more of a point-winning stroke. In recent years the service has been developed enormously, especially by the Asian players. Even when internationals are playing against each other it is not uncommon to see a player with a very good service winning as many as seven points in a game through his services not being returned. It is quite probable that the receiver could return the ball onto the opposite side of the table, but it is important for him to place the ball so that the server cannot create a winning follow-up stroke. It is mainly because of the receiver's attempted meticulous placement that errors occur. If the receiver's positioning, timing or interpretation of the spin is slightly wrong then the server has produced a stroke which usually results in the return being placed high or into the net. If the ball is returned high the server usually plays an attacking stroke and often wins the point.

So far we have noticed two aims of serving in modern table tennis. The main aim is to win the point and the secondary aim, if the main aim fails, is to position the ball so that a good follow-up stroke can be played. The type of serve used will often depend on the style of the opponent. However, no matter what service is used a player should serve so that the receiver's return cannot cause excess movement for the server during the follow-up stroke and result in an unbalanced body position. Really the service is like the opening moves in a game of chess in that it lays a foundation for the rest of the point. Depending on the opposition, a player will generally use a service which is directed to a point on the table where the opponent is forced to use his weakest stroke and therefore prevent him from gaining too much initiative during the rally. At the same time the server will try to use a service with a type of spin imparted on the ball so that the return has a good chance of being directed to a certain portion of the table. The server will have practised this serve for many hours and also the variation of follow-up strokes depending on where the return is made.

There are defensive and offensive players, left-handed and right-handed players, forehand dominating and backhand dominating players, so it is very necessary that an accomplished player can perform services with all types of spin and speed to different parts of the table so that he can play on the weaknesses of all opponents. A simple example of the importance of a variation of service can be indicated by a right-handed player who prefers to play a counter attacking game and he often becomes involved in this type of rally by serving fast down the right-handed opponent's backhand so that he is likely to play a backhand counter attacking stroke. If the server was playing a left-handed opponent and he tried the same service he would be serving to the opponent's forehand and this might result in that player doing a loop drive and so causing the server to 'block' rather than play the counter attacking game that he prefers. Therefore, it is very important that the server can make a good fast service down the line as well as across the diagonal so that he can play on the left-handed player's backhand.

Deceiving the opponent

Services are made with either the backhand or forehand side of the racket and they consist of either topspin, backspin, sidespin or a combination of topspin and sidespin or backspin and sidespin. The spin imparted on the ball will depend upon the preparation, contact and follow-through of the racket with the ball.

The most important aspect of serving is being able to deceive the opponent without breaking any of the laws on serving. Obviously, a player needs to practise services so as to obtain the length, direction, speed and spin which he requires, but all the time he should be concentrating on having almost the same preparation for a particular service as he would have for another service which may be completely different in either spin, speed, direction or length. It is the ability to change the direction of the racket when about to make contact with the ball that often produces a good service. The nearer to contact with the ball that the racket direction can be changed, the less time the opponent has to interpret the spin, speed, direction and length of the ball.

The way in which a player grips the racket when serving can alter the amount of spin imparted on the ball, the speed of the racket and the speed in the change of direction of the racket. The penhold grip allows more flexibility in the wrist joint when serving and consequently greater ranges of movement with quicker changes in direction. Shake hands grip players try to increase their range of movements in the wrist joint when serving by placing the hand further down the racket handle or by loosening or changing the position of their fingers around the handle (Fig. 1).

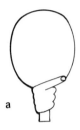
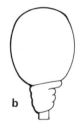
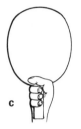
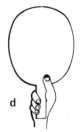

| Backhand surface of the racket | Backhand surface of the racket | Forehand surface of the racket | Forehand surface of the racket |

Shake hands grip

Shake hands grip
Hand lowered down the racket

Shake hands grip

Shake hands grip
Fingers lowered down the side of the handle

Fig. 1

In Fig. 1d, the thumb points further down the blade of the racket and the fingers point more down the side of the racket handle.

The ball can be contacted in many places by many parts of the racket to produce a similar type of spin. The more skilled a player becomes in his ability to make a similar serve by using different parts of the racket and hitting different parts of the ball then the more useful his services will become.

A player should have the ability to throw the ball up at different heights and still make the same service. The variation in the trajectory of the ball will keep the opponent guessing and possibly create an error in balance or movement.

Before releasing the ball from the hand, look carefully at the opponent's position in relation to the table. It could well be that he has taken a different ready stance because he has seen the server preparing to make a certain service and this new stance could result in the receiver gaining the initiative from the service. The server must then decide whether it is worth attempting that particular service or trying to serve to another part of the table so that the receiver has a greater distance to cover, even though it may be to a stronger department of his game (Fig. 2).

An opponent can occasionally take up a ready stance slightly closer to the table or slightly farther away than intended, so in the viewing of the opponent the server should decide what service would be most effective through the opponent's error in the preparation for the receive of service. If he takes up a stance too close to the table then a long deep service could be effective (Fig. 3b) or if he is positioned too far away from the table a short service down the forehand may be appropriate (Fig. 3c).

The actual distance of a player from the table edge in the ready stance position will depend upon his size and style of play and the above figures

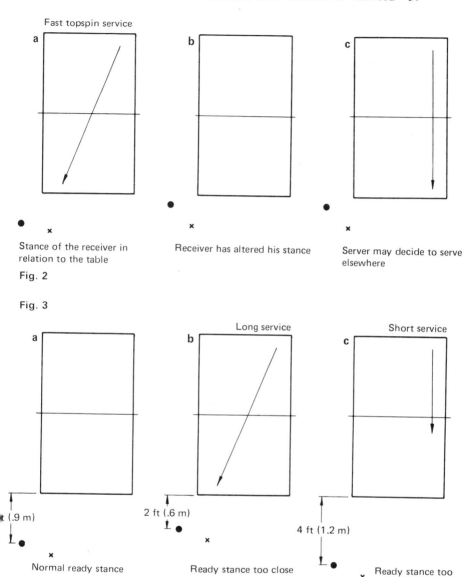

Fast topspin service

a

b

c

Stance of the receiver in
relation to the table

Fig. 2

Receiver has altered his stance

Server may decide to serve
elsewhere

Fig. 3

a

b Long service

c Short service

(.9 m)

2 ft (.6 m)

4 ft (1.2 m)

Normal ready stance

Ready stance too close
to table

Ready stance too
far away from table

are only examples. A good method to commence with is to stand one arm's
length from the edge of the table.

It may be necessary to change the service completely from a backhand to
a forehand stroke. A new serving position in relation to the table could
therefore be created and the amount of time taken to change positions
could irritate the opponent and he may not take up the ideal receive of
service position.

Fig. 4 Anatolij Strokatov, U.S.S.R., using wrist action. (1976 European Men's Singles Runner-up.)

General body movements when serving

The precise body movements will depend on the particular service being performed but there are generally three categories of body movements. Some players are very flexible in the wrist joint and they can obtain a great amount of spin on the ball through a short quick wrist action (Fig. 4). Other players use the whole of the body when serving and they build up the 'forces' through the body joints so that when contact is made with the ball the racket is travelling very fast. Some players contract different muscle groups in their body in such a manner that on movement towards the ball extra momentum is gained by a coil effect which is transferred to the racket arm (Fig. 5).

No matter what method is used when one is learning to serve, one should aim to serve the ball so that the body and toes of the leading foot are pointing in a direction common to the path of the ball. Once the ball has left the racket then one should consider the next position to move into so as to counteract the return. After one has mastered the quality of touch and body co-ordination, the really talented player can start another method of

Fig. 5 Coil effect is transferred to the racket arm. Stellan Bengtsson, Sweden. (1971 World Men's Singles Champion.)

deceiving the opponent, by serving in a direction completely alien to the direction of his body. Contact between the racket and the ball should not be made too far away from the longitudinal axis of the body, otherwise it is possible that the body will be in an unbalanced position and precision in placement of the ball will be more difficult.

Another general principle that is very important is not to have the feet too wide apart on completion of the follow-through stage of the service as this will make the recovery to the next position slower. The player should also be very careful about the length of the stroke after the ball has left the racket because he must allow himself enough time to move the racket into the correct position for the preparation of the follow-up stroke.

After stating these general principles, it is very difficult to state which is the best method of serving as many of the leading players in the world have different techniques. What can be stated is that the shake hands grip players should experiment with the 'rotary' body action and the 'spring' action and try to incorporate the wrist action in the end product.

THE RETURN OF SERVICE

Aims of the return of service

The return of a service is just as important as serving because if one cannot return well, then it usually means the point will be lost.

One can return a service in many ways. The way that you choose will often depend upon the type of player you are opposing. He may be left handed so special considerations may have to be taken into account; he may be exceptionally good on the forehand or the backhand; he may be weak at taking topspin. If you do not know your opponent's style then test him out as early as possible during the game. Although one may have the option of pushing, blocking, counter attacking, topspinning or backspinning a service, one should always concentrate on placing the ball so that the opponent becomes cramped in his style or he has to move quickly. Therefore concentrate on usually keeping the ball away from the centre area of the table and aim for a place within six inches of the end and/or side lines and preferably going away from the opponent. Ideally, try to make the ball 'break' off the side of the table.

When making contact with the ball from the server one is trying to gain the initiative but this is not always possible. If there is so much backspin on the ball and it is so short that you do not feel safe in attempting to attack it, then use a push stroke and place it. However, you should always try to think of what return the opponent can make and how you can react. Therefore it is necessary to try and return the ball so that there is sufficient spin on it and it is so short in length that the opponent can only play it back without much of an attacking stroke (Fig. 6).

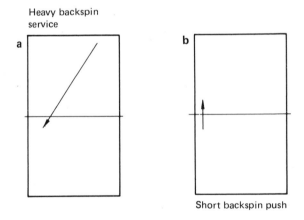

Fig. 6

Heavy backspin service

Short backspin push

Another alternative is to include speed on the push as well as spin so as to make the server hurry his second stroke and therefore give you the possible chance of gaining the initiative in the rally (Fig. 7).

Fig. 7

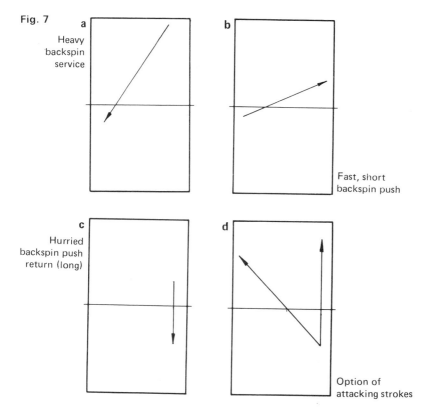

a

Heavy
backspin
service

b

Fast, short
backspin push

c

Hurried
backspin push
return (long)

d

Option of
attacking strokes

One should concentrate on being in the correct ready stance and one should aim for perfect balance and movement into the ball, with the muscles controlling the wrist joint and forearm not over-taut upon impact. The actual position in relation to the table will depend upon the player's ability and the opponent's style but the general rule for a player wishing to attack with his forehand is to be so positioned that a continuation of the backhand side line would dissect him. Always watch your opponent's position at the table; then decide if there is any possibility of him making a serve which you may not be able to receive effectively and if necessary move into a new position for the ready stance. An example of this is when playing a player who has been serving throughout the game from his backhand court and then suddenly moves across to the forehand court. You now know that he could well serve a fast ball down your forehand so you may feel insecure with your usual ready stance. You should therefore move to a new ready stance position so that your amount of movement will be reduced if he serves on your forehand. If however he does serve down your backhand it is still easy for you to play the ball diagonally to his backhand (Fig. 8).

As the player is serving one should observe the descent of the opponent's racket and the movements just before contact, on contact, and finally on follow-through. The best method is by keeping a careful eye on the wrist movements. During flight try to assess the direction, spin and speed.

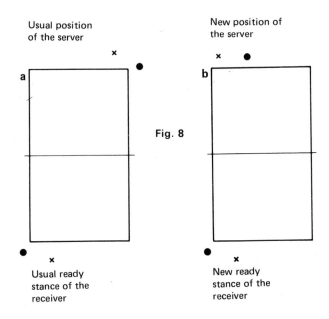

Fig. 8

Footwork for the return of service:

1 *Attacking players who prefer to use forehand strokes*
The following foot movements can be used when a player is receiving a service from the opponent's backhand court:

Fig. 9   Receive of a short service to the backhand court

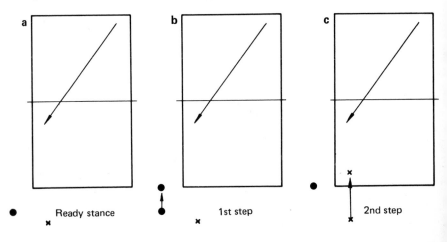

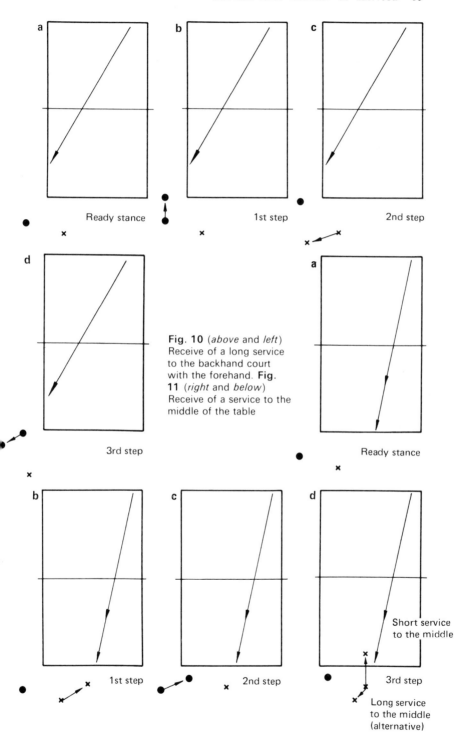

a Ready stance

b 1st step

c 2nd step

d 3rd step

Fig. 10 (*above* and *left*) Receive of a long service to the backhand court with the forehand. **Fig. 11** (*right* and *below*) Receive of a service to the middle of the table

a Ready stance

b 1st step

c 2nd step

d 3rd step

Short service to the middle

Long service to the middle (alternative)

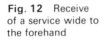

Fig. 12 Receive
of a service wide to
the forehand

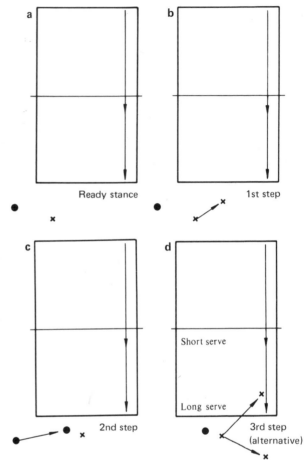

In the initial stage some players prefer to stand a little further back and as the ball is about to make contact with the opponent's racket, they start moving forward with a short two footed skipping action into the ready stance position. Further movement should not occur until the ball is moving towards the player. Once he knows the ball is going to the backhand court then the left foot will move first but if it is going to the forehand court then the right foot should be first to move. Once the player has realised in what direction the ball is travelling, he must then decide if the service will be short or long as the length of the service will determine the direction of the second and third steps.

If the service comes short to the backhand court of the table then in the second foot movement the right foot will move forward (Fig. 9). If the service comes long, the receiver could play a backhand stroke with his present footwork or move to play a forehand stroke (Fig. 10).

When the service comes down the middle of the table then with the second movement the left foot does not move towards the right foot but moves towards the backhand corner of the table and then the right foot moves forward or backwards depending on the length of the service (Fig. 11).

When the service comes down the forehand court of the table the left foot moves towards the right foot and then in the third step the right foot moves forward or backwards depending on the length of the service (Fig. 12).

As indicated in Fig. 8, if a right-handed player serves from the forehand court then the receiver will alter his ready stance. This ready stance is very similar to that of attacking players who favour backhand strokes, or players who are small in size and cannot use the other footwork.

2 *Attacking players who have strong backhand strokes*
The following foot movements can be used to return the service:

Fig. 13 Receive of a short service to the backhand court

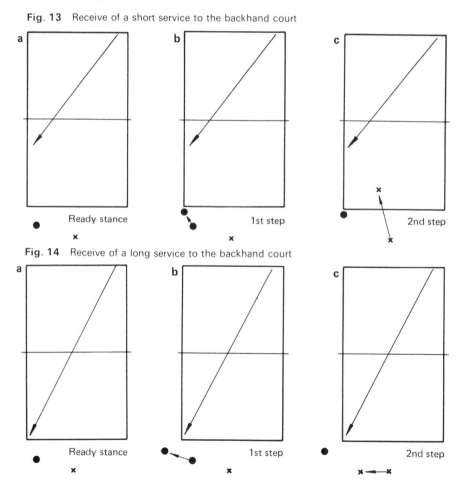

Fig. 14 Receive of a long service to the backhand court

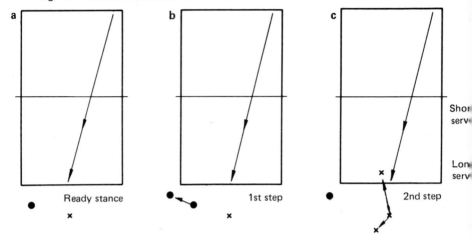

Fig. 15 Receive of a service to the middle of the table with the forehand

a — Ready stance
b — 1st step
c — 2nd step

Short service

Long service

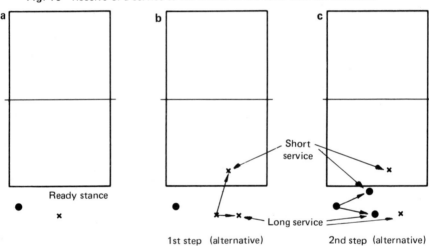

Fig. 16 Receive of a service to the middle of the table with the backhand

a — Ready stance
b — 1st step (alternative)
c — 2nd step (alternative)

Short service

Long service

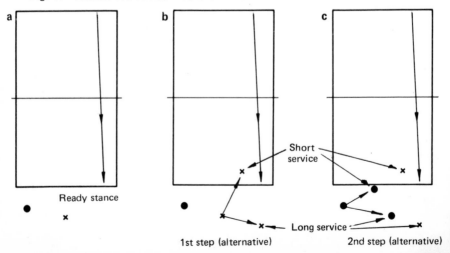

Fig. 17 Receive of a service wide to the forehand

a — Ready stance
b — 1st step (alternative)
c — 2nd step (alternative)

Short service

Long service

Although there is not so much movement involved with this type of footwork a player must be very careful not to be caught in a position where his feet are too far apart, otherwise he will experience difficulty in moving in the next required direction. The player will not receive the ball so often with his forehand in the backhand court because excessive movement will be involved. The first foot movement regarding the receive of service, follows the same general principles as the footwork for the receive of service by players who prefer to use forehand strokes. An exception is when the service comes down the middle of the table; the player then has an option of which foot to move first, depending on whether he wants to play a backhand or forehand stroke. If he wants to play a forehand, he moves his left foot first and for a backhand he will move his right foot first (Figs. 15 and 16).

3 Defensive players
Defensive players' footwork for the receive of the short service is very similar to that of the attacking player who favours the stance nearer to the middle of the table. With the long services the following footwork could be used if the player wishes to use backspin strokes.

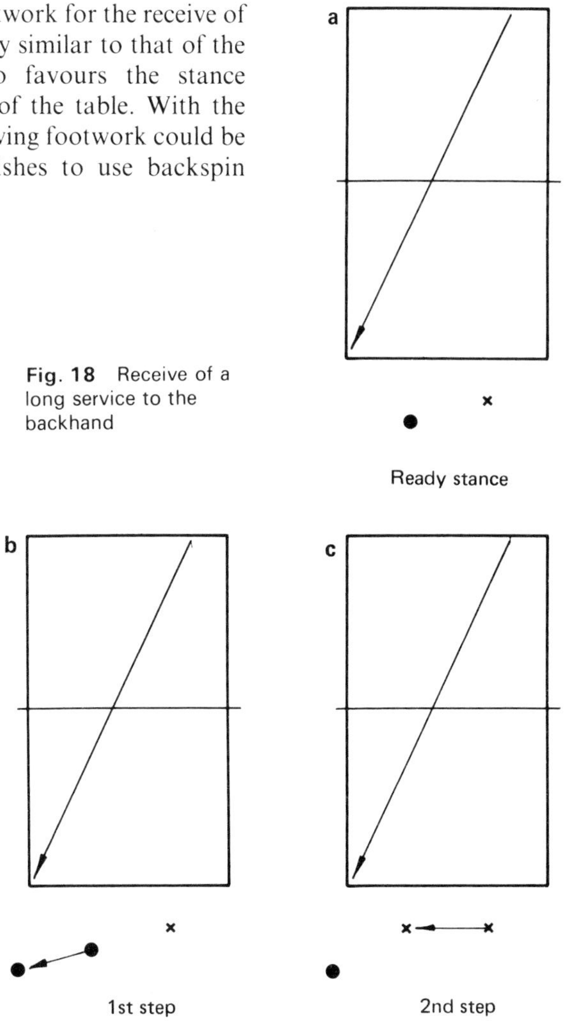

Fig. 18   Receive of a long service to the backhand

Ready stance

1st step

2nd step

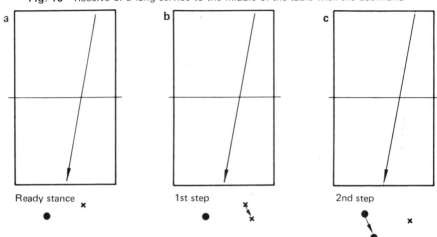

Fig. 19 Receive of a long service to the middle of the table with the backhand

Fig. 20 Receive of a long service to the middle of the table with the forehand. This receive of the service is likely to be played against service coming from the opponent's forehand court

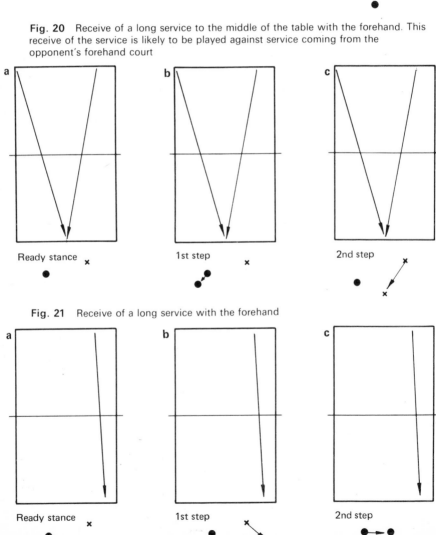

Fig. 21 Receive of a long service with the forehand

Important points regarding the return of the service

It is sometimes possible to anticipate the direction and length of the service so that the receiver can move early and therefore gain an advantage but this can be a very dangerous ploy especially if the server can conceal the direction of the service until the very last moment.

Younger players who are lacking in height and females who often lack the dynamic movement of the male are often encouraged to use the ready stance of a player who prefers to dominate with his forehand. Many players have suffered in the past because they have been coached in footwork which is not suitable to their physique or style of game. After the adolescent growth spurt, a player may be able to change to that of a forehand dominating player if his strength and height have increased.

4 Stroke Combinations for Beginners, Intermediate and Advanced Players

THE BEGINNERS STAGE

It is essential that a player learns the correct techniques involved in producing a stroke at the earliest opportunity. Once he has an understanding of the correct grip and stance required for his particular style of play, he should ensure that with each stroke he is moving his body in the most economical fashion to produce the required amount of spin, speed and direction on the ball. Movement of the feet should not be excessive at this level until the player has a complete understanding of what each part of his body is supposed to be doing during the preparation and follow-through of each stroke. Although the direction of the racket during the build up, contact with the ball, and the follow-through of the stroke is essential, the player must also realise that the movement of the arm alone is not sufficient to produce power in the stroke or consistency and accuracy in the placement of the ball. The best way of learning a stroke is to have practices which involve one player using a stroke against another player who consistently returns the ball with a stroke that is likely to be played in a game. At the beginners stage they are each learning one stroke instead of combining two or more of their own strokes in the same rally. The movement that will be necessary will be minimal in comparison with 'pressure play'* practices and this will provide a better opportunity to learn the basic principles involved in the stroke. A player may become bored during the learning of the correct technique of a stroke so he or his coach should try to set challenges regarding the number of successful strokes and the accuracy in placing the ball.

To commence with, players should concentrate on learning the push, backspin and topspin services, return of service, counter attacking strokes and the forehand smash. When they have become reasonably efficient with these strokes, simple stroke combinations can commence but footwork should be limited. An example of this is with pushing strokes where both players use forehand and backhand strokes alternately but the players try to direct the ball to a place on the table where the opponent needs to move a minimal distance (Fig. 5a(i)). When these combinations of strokes have

---

* 'Pressure play' Practices on the table that involve fast movements over different distances in different directions.

become reasonably efficient, players should progress to learning the forehand loop drive (at the beginners stage a stroke which imparts topspin will suffice), the block and the backspin defence. Stroke combinations are similarly introduced, then the length of the return is varied, then the direction.

To make stroke production a little easier in the beginners stage the player should play each particular stroke at the same contact point in relation to the height of the bounce of the ball and he should concentrate on varying the follow-through of the stroke to alter the length of the return. The speed and spin on the ball should be negligible at the beginning and only be built up as consistency improves.

For each stroke it is best to return the ball in a diagonal direction, then down the side line of the table, then in a straight line from the middle and finally in a diagonal line to the corners, from the centre of the table. Do not try to play a forehand stroke down the diagonal or middle from the backhand court until all the other exercises have been attempted.

The technique in playing each stroke has already been described in Chapter 2, but the direction of the feet and shoulders in relation to the table will depend on whether one is playing down the diagonal or side lines of the table and from where on the table one is playing the stroke. The general rules for forehand strokes are to have the feet positioned so that the lateral view of the shoulder of the non-racket arm is facing in the direction of where the ball is intended to travel, so that the racket is moving towards the ball in the line in which the ball will be played. The body should be well balanced and the elbow of the racket arm should not be cramped into the side of the body. The rear foot should be the right foot with the right-handed player and it should be angled at about 90° to the intended flight-path of the ball.

Compare Fig. 1a which depicts a forehand attacking stroke down the diagonal line of the table from the forehand court with Fig. 1b which shows a forehand down the sidelines of the table.

Figs. 1c and 1d indicate the position of the shoulders when playing a forehand stroke from the middle of the table. It is the same for a penhold or shake hands grip player.

Fig. 1e indicates a forehand stroke down the diagonal line of the table from the backhand court while Fig. 1f shows a forehand down the sideline of the table from the backhand court.

With the backhand counter attack and block the footwork variation involved in playing to different parts of the table is much less. The important point to remember is that the player should align his feet and shoulders in the direction in which he intends to play the ball.

Fig. 1a

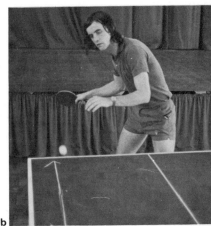

Fig. 1b

Fig. 1c

Fig. 1d

Fig. 1e

Fig. 1f

Figs. 1a–f Positions for forehand strokes (see page 73)

The following training exercises could be used in the beginners stage:

Fig. 2

Key to diagrams:

FH   Forehand strokes   BH   Backhand strokes

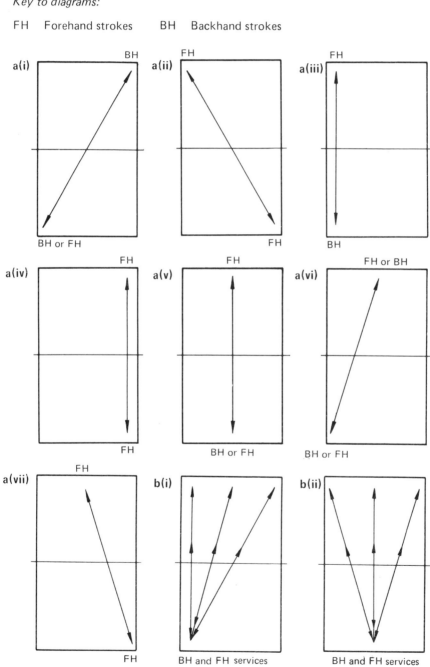

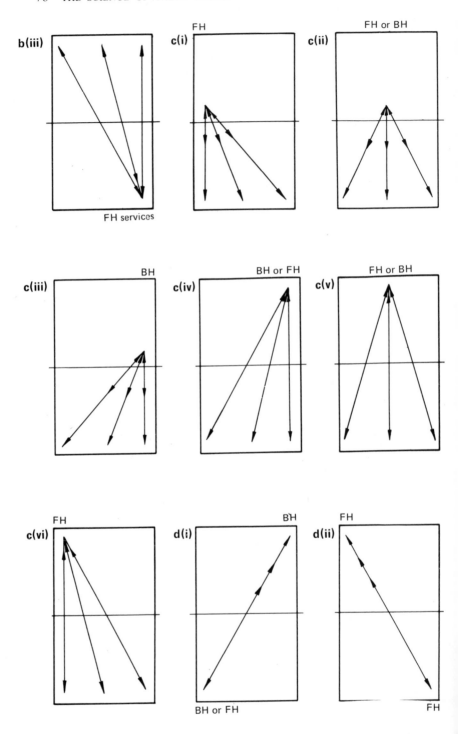

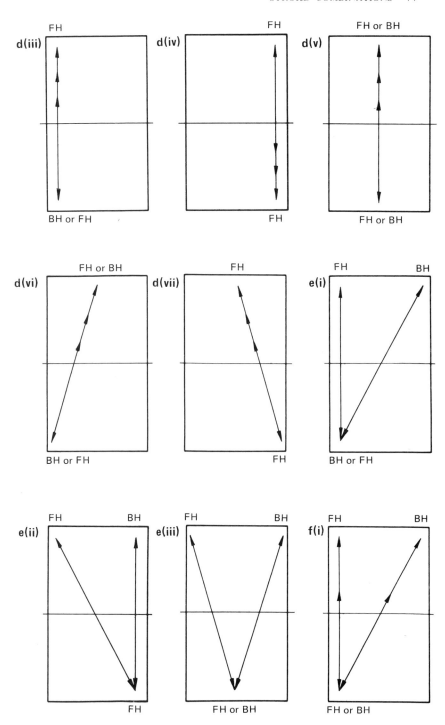

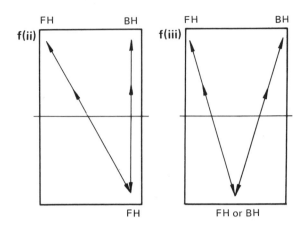

Push strokes
a(i) to a(vii), d(i) to d(vi), e(i) to e(iii), f(i) to f(iii).

Backspin services
b(i) to b(iii).

Topspin services
b(i) to b(iii).
It is difficult to serve short with topspin services. Therefore this skill should be left, as with the sidespin service, until the intermediate stage.

Receive of service
c(i) to c(vi).
Short backspin services should be pushed and topspin services should be counter attacked and chopped in the beginners stage. With these practices, the receiver can start to learn counter attack and backspin strokes.

Counter attacking strokes
a(i) to a(vii), d(i) to d(vii), e(i) to e(iii), f(i) to f(iii).

Forehand smash
a(i) to a(iii), a(v) to a(vii)
In practising this stroke it is helpful if the opponent returns the ball high after he has made a number of counter attacking or defensive strokes. A player should be capable of forehand smashing the ball to anywhere on the table from any position, when it is at a sufficient height.

Forehand loop drive
a(i) to a(iii), a(v) to a(vii), d(i) to d(iii), d(v) to d(vii), e(i) to e(iii), f(i) to f(iii).

Block
a(i) to a(iii), a(v) to a(vii), d(i) to d(iii), d(v) to d(vii), e(i) to e(iii), f(i) to f(iii).

Backspin defence
a(i) to a(iii), a(v) to a(vii), d(i) to d(iii), d(v) to d(vii), e(i) to e(iii), f(i) to f(iii).

THE INTERMEDIATE STAGE

The player should now have the ability to develop his skills in table tennis by learning the more difficult strokes and services. The sidespin topspin and sidespin backspin services, backhand loop, backhand smash, forehand sidespin loop and topspin lob strokes can all be learnt with similar practices to the strokes used in the beginners stage. He must learn the technique of imparting sidespin on the ball and also learn to combine different strokes over a wider range of movement. The degree of movement will be more excessive than in the beginners stage; therefore the footwork practices are essential so that the player is in the correct position to play a stroke. In a game situation the player only has a few hundredths of a second to decide on the direction and spin of the oncoming ball and then move into the correct position. To position himself correctly a player will have to be able to move diagonally, backward or forward. It may also be impossible to meet the ball at the same contact point for a particular stroke, so it is necessary for a player to practise playing strokes before the ball reaches the top of its bounce, also as it reaches the top of its bounce and as it descends after it has reached the top of its bounce. A player must also learn to vary the speed on the ball so he must practise soft, medium and hard strokes. Players should always commence by playing slow, controlled strokes.

The following training exercises could be used in the intermediate stage:
Key – 1, 2, 3, 4 etc. – The position of the placement of the ball on the table.

Forehand practices for side to side movement, control and consistency

Fig. 3

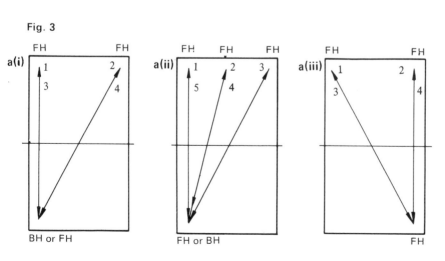

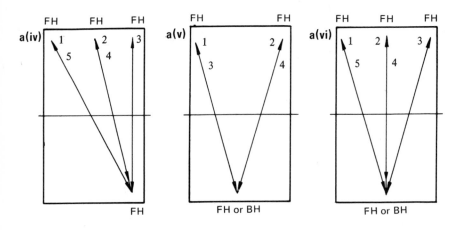

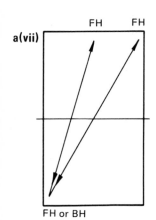

Backhand practices for side to side movement, control and consistency

Fig. 4 (*below*)

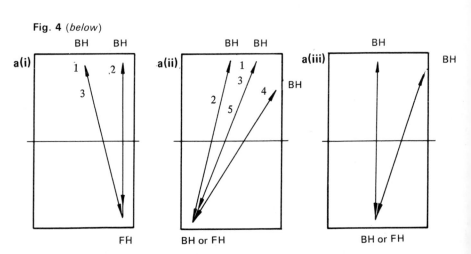

Backhand practices for consistency

These are being performed as the opponent is practising his side to side movement skills. (Figs. 3a(i), a(ii), a(v), a(vi) and a(vii).)

Backhand and forehand stroke combination practices for side to side movement, control and consistency

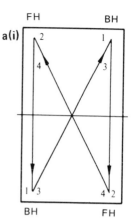

Fig. 5

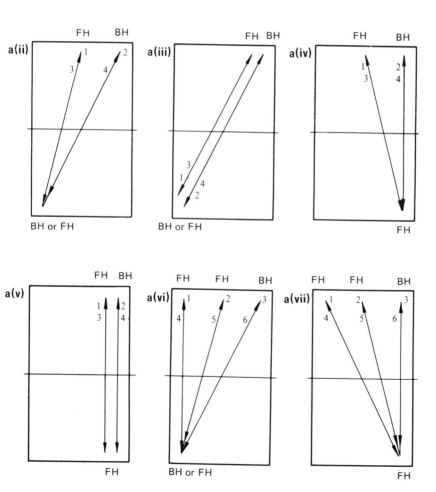

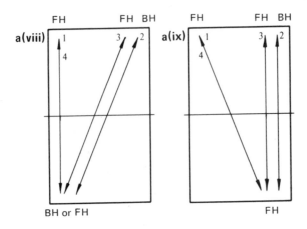

Practices for speed

Practices for speed of the stroke can be similar to those of consistency play. A player should set a target to achieve with each stroke and then see if he can play the chosen number of repetitions at a slow speed, a medium speed and finally at a fast speed. When he has become proficient with these sequences he should then try to play a smaller number of slow, medium and fast strokes but keep repeating the sequence in the same rally.

Practices for the length of the stroke

Once again the same sequences can be used but this time targets are placed on the table at different distances from the net. An example is given in Fig. 6.

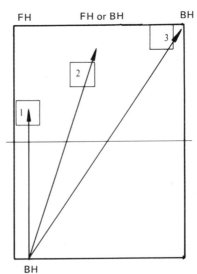

Fig. 6

Practices for different timings of the ball

As in the practices for the speed of the stroke the player decides on a number of balls he will play at a certain timing point and eventually he will play different timing points in the same rally. Examples of what is meant by early timing, peak timing and late timing:

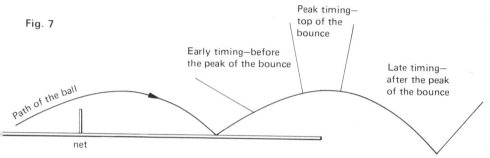

Fig. 7

Practices for strokes played at different distances from the table

These sequences involve movements over far greater distances and in many different directions. Both players should concentrate on performing these exercises with a slow, consistent stroke that is accurate in direction and imparts little spin or speed onto the ball. The variation of direction, speed, spin and length of stroke should be left to the advanced stage. There are numerous exercises which players can practise to suit their own style of play. Once the following exercises are being achieved with a good degree of success over a wide range of strokes a player should be approaching a high level of performance.

Fig. 8

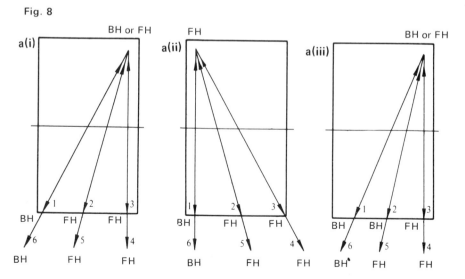

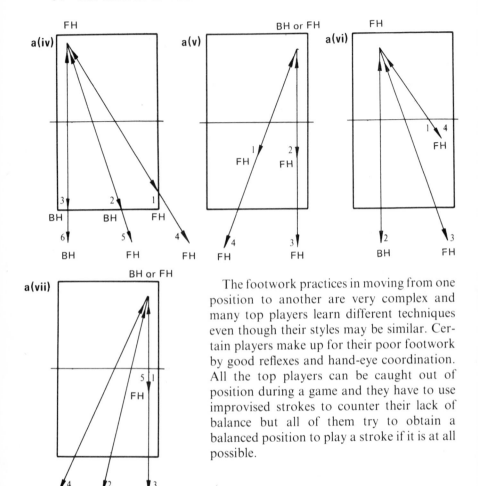

The footwork practices in moving from one position to another are very complex and many top players learn different techniques even though their styles may be similar. Certain players make up for their poor footwork by good reflexes and hand-eye coordination. All the top players can be caught out of position during a game and they have to use improvised strokes to counter their lack of balance but all of them try to obtain a balanced position to play a stroke if it is at all possible.

THE ADVANCED STAGE

During the beginners and intermediate stages all the exercises were very predictable. This meant that the player knew where the return of the ball was going and he was moving in the required direction before the ball left the opponent's racket. The rhythm of the movements was also predictable, as the player rarely had to move rapidly in a continuing zig-zag formation. Further, all the exercises had stressed consistency in a high number of repetitive movements. In the advanced stage, exercises must be practised so that the player does not always know where the ball will be travelling and he must be able to play strokes that vary in direction, length, timing, speed and spin.

A player should now be concentrating on practising sequences where he tries to win the point from the service, return of service, third, fourth and fifth stroke, because in many matches over 75 per cent of points are won before the sixth stroke of the rally. A high level of physical fitness is a very important requirement for performing exercises well in the advanced stage. Pressure play exercises on the table as well as physical conditioning in the gymnasium can be used to develop stamina and mobility in the individual. There are many permutations of exercises that could be practised but it is at this stage in a player's development that he must make a critical self-assessment of his own game. He should then create exercises that will both improve his strengths and eradicate weaknesses. The following English international players included these practices on training camps between 1974 and 1976 when I was trainer/coach to the England team.

Desmond Douglas (England No. 1, European No. 5, World No. 7)
Desmond is a left-handed attacking player who has very good backhand strokes. He has good reflexes and flexibility and he has a remarkable hand-eye coordination that allows him to have a very good timing with the ball. He is also very agile and he moves very quickly when in a position close to the table. He lacks the ability to impart vicious spin on his services but his return of service is very good. He is comparatively weak when caught in a position away from the table or when stretched wide to the forehand. He also lacks power in smashing against the high topspin lob defence and he does not like playing against consistent flighted topspin. Like all the other English players it was necessary to try and rectify his weaknesses so that he could create a position to dominate with his strongest strokes.

PRACTICES: Service practice (Fig. 10a(i)). Receive of service practice (Figs. 10a(ii)–(iv)). Service and follow-up practice (Figs. 10a(v)–(viii)), known as a third ball attack. Receive of service and follow-up practice (Figs. 10a(ix)–(xii)), known as a fourth ball attack. Service, placement and follow-up. (Figs. 10a(xiii)–(xviii)), known as a fifth ball attack. General weakness practice (Figs. 10a(xix–xx)).

Nicky Jarvis (England No. 1, European No. 14, World No. 32 in 1976)
Before a serious back injury in 1976, from which he has only just recovered, Nicky was one of the finest players in the world against defensive players. He is an attacking player who has a very good loop drive and a wide variety of accurate services. His main weaknesses are his backhand attack and his receive of the service short and wide to the forehand.

PRACTICES: Service practice (Fig. 10b(i)). Receive of service practice (Figs. 10b(ii)–(iv)). Third ball attack (Figs. 10b(v)–(vii)). Fourth ball attack (Figs. 10b(viii)–(xi)). Fifth ball attack (Figs. 10b(xii)–(xvi)). General weakness practice (Figs. 10b(xviii)–(xx)).

Fig. 9 Jill Hammersley (*left*) and Linda Howard, England (European Women's Doubles Champions). Jill was also the 1976 European Women's Singles Champion

Paul Day (1976 European Boys' Doubles Champion)

Paul is a left-handed attacking player with a very good variation of forehand services and forehand loop drives. He has a good physique and he is very quick in his movements around the table. He uses his fitness and mobility to try and move into positions so that he can dominate the game with his forehand strokes. His backhand attacking strokes are weak and he is vulnerable when receiving short services and when playing against good defensive players.

PRACTICES: Service practice (Fig. 10c(i)). Receive of service practice (Figs. 10c(ii)–(iv)). Third ball attack (Figs. 10c(v)–(vii)). Fourth ball attack (Figs. 10c(viii)–(xi)). Fifth ball attack (Figs. 10c(xiii)–(xvi)). General weakness practice (Figs. 10c(xvii)–(xviii)).

Jill Hammersley (1976 European Women's Singles Champion)

Jill won the Ladies Singles and the Ladies Doubles, partnered by Linda Howard, in the European Championships in Prague in 1976 (Fig. 9). She is one of the best defensive players in the world but she can also attack very well with her backhand against the push ball. She has a weakness against players who can notice her variation of defensive strokes and who keep looping the ball with high heavy topspin. She is also weak if she tries to attack with her forehand against defensive players who place every ball down her forehand.

PRACTICES: Service practice (Fig. 10d(i)). Receive of service practice (Figs. 10d(ii)–(iii)). Third ball attack (Figs. 10d(iv)–(vi)). Fourth ball attack (Figs. 10d(vii)–(x)). Fifth ball attack (Figs. 10d(xi)–(xv)). General weakness practice (Figs. 10d(xvi)–(xix)).

Carol Knight (1977 English Open Women's Singles Champion)

Carol is an attacking player who has one of the finest forehand loop drives in women's table tennis. She has a good variation of services and her backhand loop drive is improving rapidly. Once she has improved her level of physical fitness she is capable of reaching a standard comparable with the best women players in the world. Carol is weak against players who can involve her in long counter attacking rallies or players who can loop continuously against her.

PRACTICES: Service practice (Fig. 10e(i)). Receive of service practice (Figs. 10e(ii)–(iii)). Third ball attack (Figs. 10e(iv)–(vi)). Fourth ball attack (Figs. 10e(vii)–(x)). Fifth ball attack (Figs. 10e(xii)–(xv)). General weakness practice (Figs. 10e(xvi)–(xxi)).

There are numerous exercises that can be practised which will develop stamina, power and mobility in the individual. These exercises involve rapid movement over a short time in a conditioned or unconditioned direction. The following examples could be practised.

In Fig. 11a the player must play forehand counter attacking strokes from position one, then position two, then he must move and touch the net post on the right side of the table with his racket; he must then return to position one and continue the sequence until an error is made. The opponent should stand about two yards away from the table and play slow backhand counter attacking strokes alternatively to positions one and two. As the opponent improves, 'the feeder'* can stand closer to the table or increase the speed of his stroke so that the player who is using the forehand strokes has less time in which to move.

In Fig. 11b the practice is similar except that the player touches the net post on the left side of the table with his left hand, and the feeder uses a forehand counter attacking stroke.

In Fig. 11c the player pushes the ball then moves back to touch a marker on the floor approximately ten feet from the edge of the table; he must then return to push the next return and the sequence continues until a mistake occurs. The feeder pushes the ball slow and high at the beginning and he increases the speed of the return as the player improves in his movements about the table. The player can push the ball with the backhand or forehand and he can touch the marker with his racket or his left hand. The actual stroke and touching of the marker will depend upon the position of

---

* 'The feeder': The player who is placing the ball so that the opponent can practise a certain sequence.

the ball on the table from the feeder. This exercise is very useful for defensive players, and the top players can place the marker more than ten feet from the end of the table.

In Fig. 11d three markers are placed on the floor and numbered one, two and three. As the feeder serves or pushes the ball, he calls out one of the marker numbers. The player must then push the ball and move to touch that marker with either his racket or left hand and then return to a position so that he can push the next stroke and move to the next or same position, that the feeder may call.

A good practice for players is that of placing the ball towards the right hip of the opponent. Many players have difficulty in moving their feet so that the body is to the side of the oncoming ball when they play a forehand stroke. They must move to allow their right arm to make the correct approach towards the ball. Therefore after a player has looped the ball the opponent should try and work out where the player's recovery stance will be and then block the ball towards his right hip. This practice is excellent for developing precision in the stroke of the feeder and feet movements of the looping player.

Key to diagrams

BH = Backhand   L   = Loop
FH = Forehand   S   = Smash
T   = Topspin   P   = Push
ST = Sidespin topspin CA = Counter attack
SB = Sidespin backspin B   = Block
F   = Flick

Fig. 10 Practice sequences used for specific players. See pages 85–9

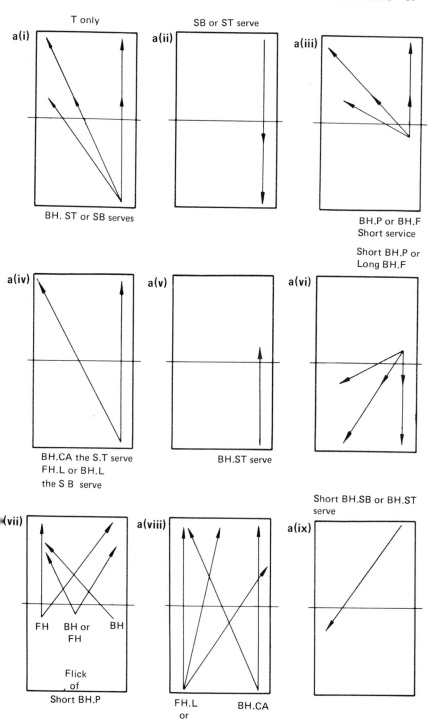

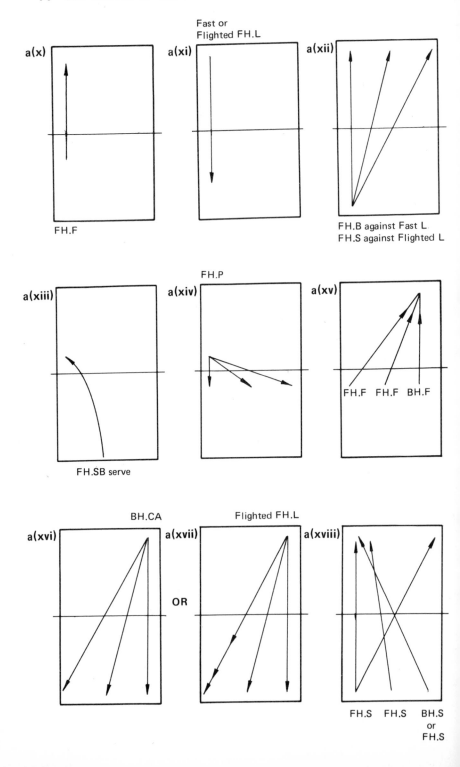

a(x)

a(xi)

Fast or
Flighted FH.L

a(xii)

FH.F

FH.B against Fast L
FH.S against Flighted L

a(xiii)

a(xiv)

FH.P

a(xv)

FH.SB serve

FH.F   FH.F   BH.F

a(xvi)

BH.CA

a(xvii)

Flighted FH.L

a(xviii)

OR

FH.S   FH.S   BH.S
or
FH.S

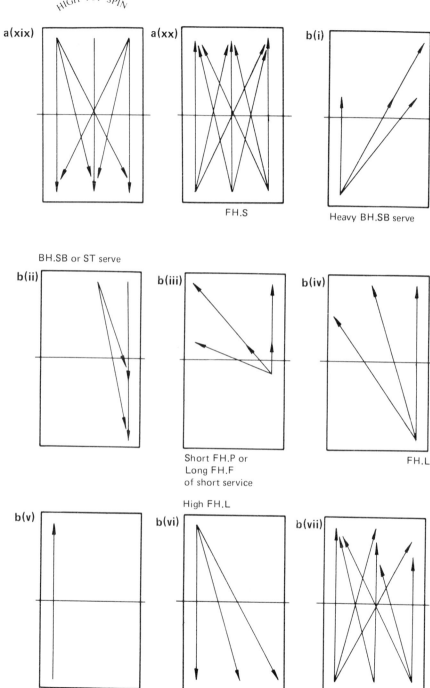

HIGH TOP SPIN

a(xix)

a(xx)

FH.S

b(i)

Heavy BH.SB serve

BH.SB or ST serve

b(ii)

b(iii)

Short FH.P or
Long FH.F
of short service

b(iv)

FH.L

High FH.L

b(v)

BH.SB serve

b(vi)

b(vii)

FH.S

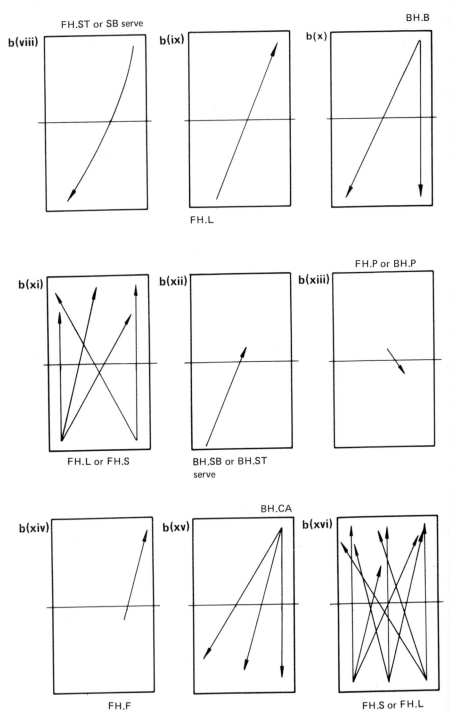

FH.ST or SB serve

b(viii)

b(ix)

BH.B

b(x)

FH.L

b(xi)

b(xii)

FH.P or BH.P

b(xiii)

FH.L or FH.S

BH.SB or BH.ST
serve

BH.CA

b(xiv)

b(xv)

b(xvi)

FH.F

FH.S or FH.L

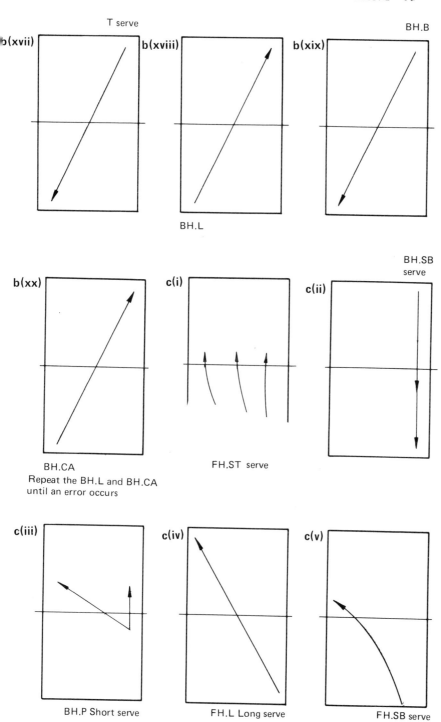

b(xvii) T serve

b(xviii)

b(xix) BH.B

BH.L

b(xx)

c(i)

c(ii) BH.SB serve

BH.CA
Repeat the BH.L and BH.CA
until an error occurs

FH.ST serve

c(iii)

c(iv)

c(v)

BH.P Short serve

FH.L Long serve

FH.SB serve

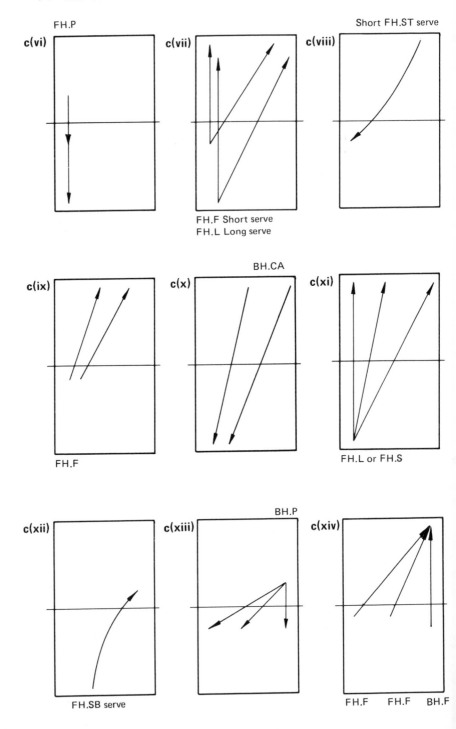

FH.P

c(vi)

c(vii)

Short FH.ST serve

c(viii)

FH.F Short serve
FH.L Long serve

c(ix)

BH.CA

c(x)

c(xi)

FH.F

FH.L or FH.S

c(xii)

BH.P

c(xiii)

c(xiv)

FH.SB serve

FH.F   FH.F   BH.F

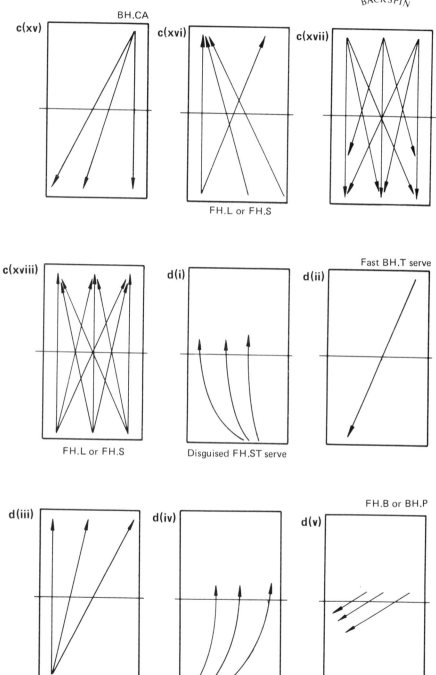

c(xv) BH.CA

c(xvi) FH.L or FH.S

c(xvii)

c(xviii) FH.L or FH.S

d(i) Disguised FH.ST serve

d(ii) Fast BH.T serve

d(iii) BH. Backspin or Float

d(iv) FH.ST serve

d(v) FH.B or BH.P

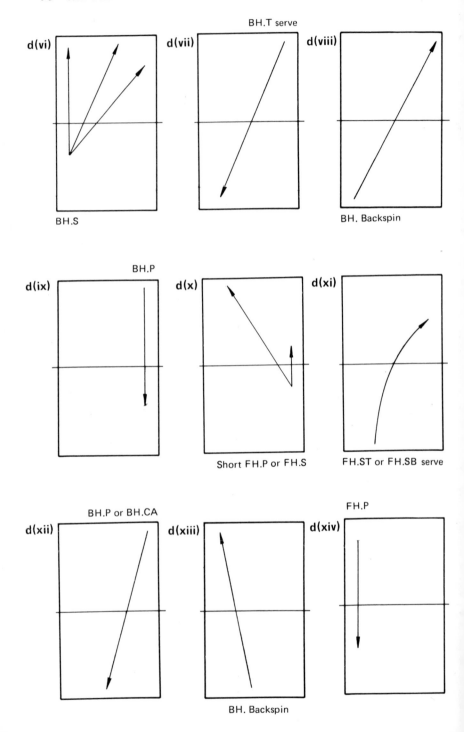

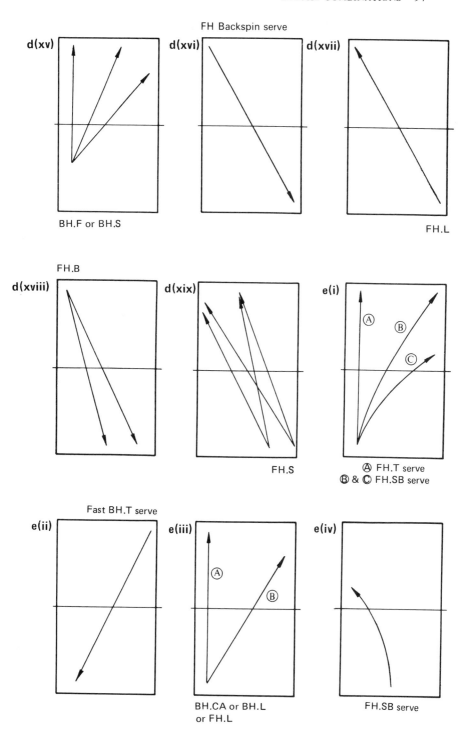

FH Backspin serve

d(xv)

BH.F or BH.S

d(xvi)

d(xvii)

FH.L

FH.B

d(xviii)

d(xix)

FH.S

e(i)

Ⓐ FH.T serve
Ⓑ & Ⓒ FH.SB serve

Fast BH.T serve

e(ii)

e(iii)

BH.CA or BH.L
or FH.L

e(iv)

FH.SB serve

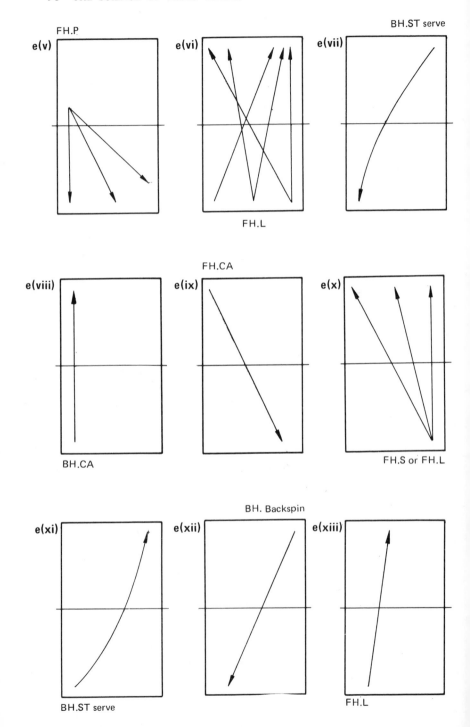

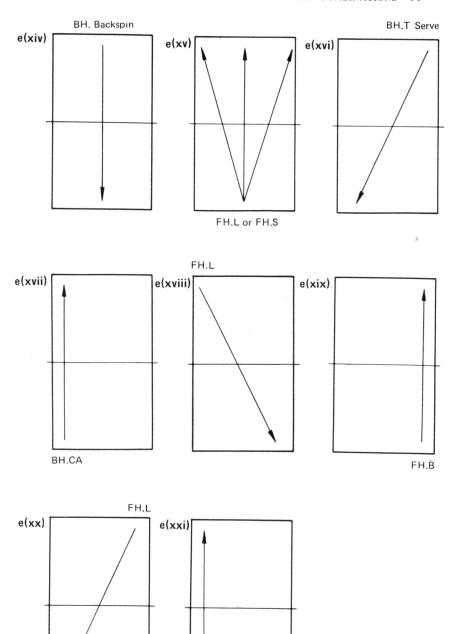

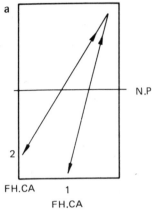

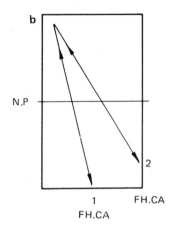

Fig. 11

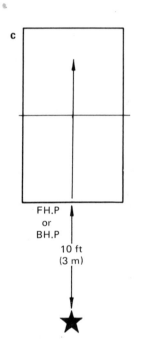

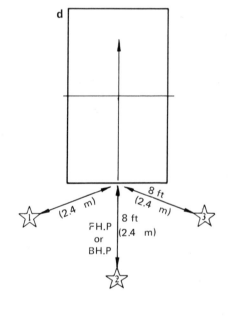

5 Doubles

There are no doubles matches in the World or European Men's Team Championships, but the Women's Doubles match can often decide the outcome of the Women's Team Championships. In the World and European Men's Championships there are three players a side, each playing a maximum of three singles sets, and the first team to win five sets will win the match. However, in the World or European Women's Team Championships, there may be two, three or four players participating on one team. The match will consist of a maximum of four singles and one doubles set. An outstanding lady player on any one team can almost win the match entirely by herself, as she can play in three of the five sets.

The most important team matches for European players besides the championships previously mentioned are the European Super League matches. In this league, doubles sets account for two of the seven sets played. If a team can win the Men's Doubles and the Mixed Doubles they can gain overall victory by winning only two of the remaining five singles sets. Between 1974 and 1976 English teams usually won most of their doubles sets in the European League, with the pairings of Desmond Douglas and Denis Neale (1977 World Doubles Quarter Finalists) and Desmond Douglas and Linda Howard (former European Youth Champions and 1978 English Open Champions).

The Men's Doubles, Women's Doubles and Mixed Doubles competitions in major tournaments are coveted titles and are very prestigious for the players and their associations. Therefore, when choosing a doubles combination, whether for World, European or domestic events, selectors must realise that it is possible that their best two players at singles may not be as good a doubles partnership as another pair of lower-ranked players.

Players have contrasting styles and it is very difficult to state what is the best combination of styles for doubles play because much will depend upon the techniques of their opponents. When analysing successful doubles combinations in England, it is noticeable that there is a marked contrast in their playing styles. Desmond Douglas and Denis Neale can be classified as a counter attacking combination, whereas the partnership of Paul Day and Andrew Barden (1976 European Boys Doubles Champions) can be classified as a topspin loop drive combination. Jill Hammersley and Linda Howard (1976 European Women's Doubles Champions) form a defensive and counter attacking combination. In Europe, two of the most successful doubles combinations over the past seven years were Stellan Bengtsson and Kjell Johansson (Sweden), a topspin loop drive and counter attacking combination, and Dragutin Surbek and Anton Stipancic (Yugoslavia), a topspin loop drive combination.

A study of these Men's Doubles pairs shows that they all have a familiar characteristic of one player being right-handed and the other, left-handed. The players also have very strong forehand topspin loop drives and/or forehand smashes. Usually the players with the stronger forehand topspin loop drives have weaker backhand strokes. This is because during a game of singles they have been coached to try and dominate the rallies with their stronger forehand strokes. Dragutin Surbek and Paul Day are very good examples of forehand topspin loop drive players.

The big advantage of a right- and left-handed doubles pair is that they find it easier to play a ball from the middle area of their side of the table, with their more powerful forehand strokes. Also, after they have played a service or stroke, they can usually move out to the same side of the table throughout the match and so leave the whole area behind the table free, for their partner to play the next stroke (Fig. 1).

Fig. 1 Doubles pair – with right-handed and left-handed players

When two right-handed players or two left-handed players are partnering each other, they are more likely to be restricted in their movements about the table. The players may move in a sequence like the left-handed and right-handed combination, or they can move in a circular system, either clockwise or anti-clockwise. Partners who prefer to serve and dominate with their backhand strokes are likely to move in a clockwise direction (Fig. 4a), whereas the partners who prefer to serve and dominate with their forehand strokes usually move in an anti-clockwise direction (Figs. 3a, 3b, and 4b).

Fig. 2

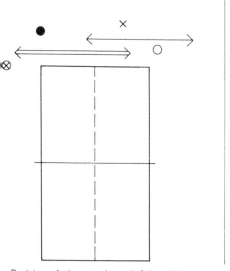

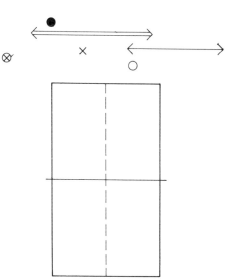

Position of players when a left-handed
player is serving or receiving the service

Position of players when a right-handed
player is serving or receiving the service

Key:
●   Left foot of left-handed player
⊕   Right foot of left-handed player
⇔ Direction of movements of left-handed player
○   Left foot of right-handed player
x   Right foot of right-handed player
⇔ Direction of movements of right-handed player

Fig. 3a (*left*) and **Fig. 3b** (*right*) Doubles pair – two right-handed players

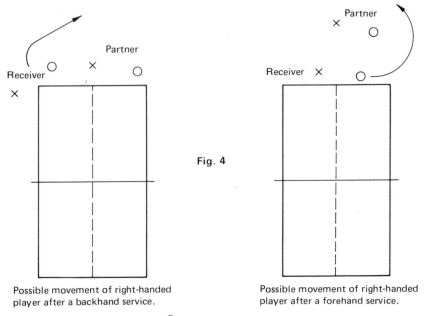

Fig. 4

Possible movement of right-handed player after a backhand service.

Possible movement of right-handed player after a forehand service.

Key: x Left foot o Right foot) Movement after the service

These partnerships may be able to follow a set sequence of movement for most of the rallies, but it is quite possible that at some stage in the set they will have to improvise upon their original sequence.

Doubles combinations depend upon close communication between the players regarding the understanding of their partners' stroke production, mental attitude and movement patterns.

Although there are exceptions to the rules, I have noticed that two players who try to win the point very quickly in singles matches do not make a successful doubles combination. In all doubles pairings there should be a player who can consistently return the ball to the opponent's side of the table. This is usually the person who will create the 'opening' for his partner to win the point by a smash or topsin loop drive.

A very important factor in doubles play is that of knowing how your partner is going to react to various situations. You must know if he will become nervous in a big tournament, or in an important match, or when the score is very close near the end of a game. It may be that he does not play his strokes so convincingly or that his body movements may be too tentative. In these situations it is important that you really understand his mental state both on and off the table so that you can have a good idea of how to help and encourage him so that he may regain composure and resume playing up to his potential.

Because the ball is being struck alternately by each player, the 'non-striking' partner must have a clear understanding of what spin his partner is imparting upon the ball so that when the opponent plays a return stroke he will be able to follow up with an effective counter stroke. The amount of spin that your partner imparts upon the ball may be completely different from that of a similar stroke from you. With plenty of match practice, the understanding of each others' strokes should increase.

Men's Doubles partnerships that depend entirely on defensive strokes are usually unsuccessful, especially against a good forehand topspin loop drive combination. This is because the attacking players have plenty of time to move into the correct position to play their strokes and to angle the ball very wide. If forehand topspin loop driving players can understand their partner's positional play, they should have plenty of time to move into position even against the counter attacking players, and if their spin variation and consistency of stroke is good then they should have a good chance of winning most of their matches. A Men's Doubles partnership of one defensive player and one attacking player is usually unsuccessful, especially against opponents who have good topspin loop drives and forehand smashes. The attacking pair often dominate the rallies and create difficulties for the opposing attacking player, who will end up blocking the ball during most of the rallies.

In the Mixed Doubles, combinations of defence and attack, and all defensive combinations, are usually unsuccessful because the opposing man of an attacking partnership can usually dominate the rallies. The most ideal partnerships are often composed of a man who has a good variation of services and a topspin loop drive, and a woman who has a good counter attacking game and can control the opponents' services and effectively block the topspin loop drive. Jacques Secretin and Claude Bergeret (France), the 1977 World Champions, are a good example of this type of combination.

In Women's Doubles the above principles regarding doubles partnerships do not really apply. Women usually lack the dynamic power of men so that attacking players cannot move about the table from one point to another so quickly. Therefore they do not always obtain a position to play continuous attacking strokes. They also do not have the same amount of power in the execution of their strokes. In Women's Doubles, therefore, an attacking-defensive or a totally defensive combination still have a good chance of being successful.

I am also of the opinion that the ideal partnership, especially in Men's Doubles, is that of one left-handed player and one right-handed player, both of whom have good counter attacking strokes and the ability to 'read' the spin on the ball and vary the spin and speed on their topspin and sidespin loop drives.

Before playing a doubles match, it is very important, as in singles, to analyse the opponents' style of play and then decide upon your tactics. It could be that your partner dislikes playing against a certain style that one of your opponents uses, so you then have to decide whether it is best for your partner to receive service from him in the first game or the second game. However, it may turn out that you have no choice in the matter, because if they win the option to serve, they may decide to give the service away and therefore choose to receive the service (see Chapter 14 page 197). If you do have the option either to serve or receive the service, then you must consider whether it is worth trying to 'catch the opponents cold' and get off to a good start by playing the apparently worst order in the first game and keep your best order until the second game and latter half of the third game. Alternatively you could play your best order in the first game and then hope to demoralise the opponents for the second game or have a good start in the third game, so leaving the opposition too big a deficit to make up when the order of serving is changed in the third game.

Many doubles partnerships help each other by using pre-arranged tactics. A simple example is that of dropping the non-racket arm below the table and making a sign to indicate what service you are going to do. Some partnerships use the sign of two fingers pointing towards the floor as meaning a sidespin topspin service, or a clenched fist which means a sidespin backspin service. This advance information can help the partner prepare for the type of return the opponent is likely to play.

During a doubles game most of the tactics in singles matches still apply. Each player should try strokes during the game that assist his partner to dominate the game. While playing your strongest strokes, you should also try to play on the opponents' weakest strokes. A good tactic is that of quickly playing the ball towards the person who last played the ball, because it means he will have to move out of the way very quickly. If he is slow in moving, then it is likely that his partner will not be in a good position to play a 'point winning' stroke. When this situation occurs, the opponents often leave a large area of their court 'open' so that you can gain the intitiative in dictating the placement of the ball during the rally.

6 World Table Tennis

A BRIEF HISTORY AND SURVEY OF WORLD TRENDS AND TACTICS

Table tennis techniques have changed considerably in the last fifty years. One needs only to read books about table tennis describing the scene in the late 1920s to envisage the majority of men playing with long trousers and pimpled rubber rackets and not really going beyond the stroke play of defence and forehand and backhand smashes.

Although sponge rackets were being developed by John Jacques and Company as early as 1927, players had limited success with them. Before 1937 certain players used to combine the effects of the 'fingerspin'* service and their sponge racket to produce some surprising results in leading competitions. Their services were almost unplayable and the rallies were usually very short. However, after 1937 the 'fingerspin' service was banned and rallies tended to become quite prolonged. By 1951 a few players who used sponge rackets were producing good results and by 1954 several Japanese players using sponge rackets were gaining world supremacy, even though Japan did not enter the World Championships until 1952. They had been using sponge rackets in internal competitions for the previous twenty years.

With the development of the sponge racket the whole game of table tennis has changed in character. Although sponge rackets as we know them today have been on the scene for over two decades the quality of the rubber has changed, and the same degree of speed and spin could not have been achieved in the past. As competition has thrived in the last twenty years, coaches all over the world have developed more and more advanced skill techniques and tactics.

The sponge racket was found to be ideal for putting tremendous spin on the ball and when it was being established in world play a point was often won by the service or, if not, by the smash which was used as the follow-up stroke. In the 1950s there was the introduction of a new stroke. It was really an exaggerated topspin where there was a greater preparation, follow-

---

* After 1937 one of the laws of table tennis stated that the ball must be projected upwards from the palm of the hand before the racket can strike the ball. Before 1937 a player could spin the ball with his fingers and then strike the ball. Different types of spin could be produced depending upon the movement of the fingers upon the ball.

through and wrist action. The ball was given a finer touch and the stroke was nearer to the vertical plane. The loop drive in its simpler form had arrived. It had most probably been first thought of because players were getting used to their opponent's services and were able to return them in such a position that the server could not follow-up with a smash. Another vicious stroke was needed which could easily win the point and the loop drive seemed the most effective. This stroke really led to the downfall of the totally defensive player. Before its introduction there had been many defensive players but they were just unable to control the greater amount of topspin and were becoming easy opposition for people whom they had previously beaten. This disheartened many defensive players and they retired. Others eventually found the control to cope with the spin, but the added advantage for the attackers with the sponge racket meant that very few major men's championships were ever won by defensive players. Attacking players also had difficulties in coping with the player who could get his loop drive in first, but they eventually learnt to block the ball effectively. Even then the chance of a good return was always difficult to predict.

The Asian penhold players demonstrated the way to counteract this 'new weapon' and they did it quite simply by intense pressure from their own serve and service return so that they could prevent the opponent getting a good loop in during a rally. They then followed up with a hard smash against a lesser degree of spin. Naturally a few of them developed loop drives as well, but they mainly relied on quick thrusting movements in the mode of hard smashes and blocks. It was not until the early 1970s that the loop drive was to find its true value against the penhold style of game.

The sidespin loop was to become more widely used and the loop drive against any style of ball from the opponent was to become very dominant. This is not to say that players would loop all the returns, but if it was necessary they could do so. The European players were moving further away from the table and therefore giving themselves more time to position themselves for the faster return ball. The European nations had been practising this style since about 1965 but it was not until the 1970s that results really began to show. The possibility of a take-over from Eastern tactical supremacy had been showing in places throughout the world since 1970, but the big day came in Nagoya (Japan) in 1971 when Stellan Bengtsson from Sweden won the World Singles Championships and many Europeans obtained good results. Eventually by 1973, in Sarajevo (Yugoslavia), seven out of the eight quarter finalists in the World Championships were Europeans, and the Men's Team Championships was won by Sweden. Although The People's Republic of China won the Swaythling Cup in Calcutta in 1975, two Europeans contested the Men's Singles final for the first time since 1953. In the 1975 final Istvan Jonyer of Hungary defeated Anton Stipancic of Yugoslavia.

The tactical reasons for these results are as follows: The new rubbers which were being produced gave much more spin and speed and the Europeans were able to stay further away from the table and so have more time available to play their strokes. Even their slow controlled strokes had sufficient top and/or sidespin on them to prevent the hard flat hitters (typical of the penhold style of play) from making outright winners. Penhold strokes gradually became blocks instead of smashes and the initiative had thus passed to the European style. Europeans merely played the heavy topspin game if they could not kill the ball from the return of service, or service, then waited for the block to be slightly weak in positioning. Then they finished it either by a smash or a fast loop drive, often with sidespin so that it 'left the opponent'. The sidespin/topspin players posed many problems to the 'blockers' because there was so much variation of speed, spin and direction. Recently in Europe this blocking game has become less effective and now players only block occasionally and try to play their own loop or smash. This results in players often looping each others' loops for long rallies and often at great distances from the table.

After the 1975 World Championships in Calcutta the Chinese were to establish themselves firmly as the leading table tennis nation in the world. During these championships one of their leading lady players, Ke Hsin-Ai, easily won most of her games in the team event. She was using a racket especially made in China, which had on one side a very thin layer of sponge and long thin pimples and on the other side a more conventional amount of rubber and sponge. Each side of the racket imparted a completely different type of spin on the ball. Because the racket surfaces were identical in colour and she kept turning the racket in her hand between strokes it was almost impossible to tell which side of the racket she was using and therefore interpreting the spin on the ball was very difficult.

Before the World Championships in Birmingham in 1977, the Chinese men's and women's teams produced players who were very skilful with these rackets and they easily beat the top European players. The European players never learnt to counteract successfully the variation of spin by 1977 and China easily won both team championships in Birmingham. The only player who really played well against the Chinese players was Mitsuru Kohno of Japan and he went on to win the World Singles title. There are different views as to why Kohno won the title and it is still uncertain if he was actually allowed to win, because the Chinese had always stressed that friendship was more important than always winning and China had already won the Men's Team Championship. However, Kohno did have more opportunity of playing the Chinese players than did the Europeans in the two years before Birmingham and the Japanese coaches instructed him to listen to the different sounds when the ball hit the two sides of the Chinese player's racket. He then interpreted these sounds into the amount of spin on the ball and therefore had more time to play his strokes than the players who waited for the ball to bounce. However, it should be noted that Kohno beat a Chinese player in the semi-final and final of the singles yet he never won a match against the Chinese team in the final of the team event!

Because of the utter confusion in the interpretation by most players of the spin on the ball, the International Table Tennis Federation have banned the rackets with excessively long pimples so the era of these players may be over but that of China will not be, as they have many players who can play with conventional rackets and still beat most of the leading players in the world.

If one ignores the tactics of the players who used the long pimpled rackets one can summarise by stating that modern tactics today are:

1 Serve so that the other person is made to do what you want him to do. In practice you should have become used to countering every variation of return from your own services.
2 Follow-up if possible with a loop drive or smash or push the ball back short. A long heavy backspin push can be effective against a penhold player who does not use the loop drive.
3 When receiving serve ensure that you try to impart heavy topspin on any long serve; push or flick the return of the short service, short, or to an awkward position for the opponent, so your follow-up stroke can be an effective attacking stroke (i.e. loop or smash). In international matches many points are won before the ball has crossed the net five times.

REVIEW OF SUCCESSFUL COUNTRIES

Men's teams

1 The People's Republic of China (World Champions)
Table tennis is the national sport in this country and there are over one million players. The overall standard is extremely high and their coaching scheme is second to none. Their coaches have carefully studied all the leading players in all other countries and after analysing their weaknesses they have developed players with different styles so that they can oppose foreigners and know they will have a good chance of winning.

In the World Championships in Birmingham they included Kuo Yao Hua, a penhold looping player, Li Chen-Shih, a fast flat hitting and blocking penhold player, and Liang Ke Liang, a shake hands grip defensive player who also had an excellent array of attacking strokes. All their players are extremely fit and have superb footwork. They are very good at following up their excellent services although there has been some criticism of their services because they sometimes impart spin on the ball during the 'throw up'.

2 *Japan (2nd in 1977 World Championships)*
The Japanese have continually gained honours in World Championships
for the last twenty years. Table tennis is very popular in their universities
and it is organised on a similar basis to collegiate sports in the United States
of America. Many of their previous international players coach within the
university system and they are all very dedicated in their work. Like the
Chinese players, most of them use the penhold grip but nearly all of them
prefer to use speed rather than excessive spin on their strokes.

Mitsuru Kohno, their current World Champion, concentrates on trying
to play the ball at an early contact point and he obtains extreme angles
when playing the ball. Unlike most European players he hits the ball very
flat. The Japanese have yet to develop a really good looping player, either
with the conventional shake hands grip or the penhold grip. They do have
an excellent defensive player in Norio Takashima and he is a very valuable
member of their team because his inclusion provides a variation of style to
the rest of the team.

3 *Sweden (3rd in 1977 World Championships)*
Unlike the Chinese and Japanese, the Swedes seem to concentrate on
producing players with one particular style of game and then they try to
ensure that techniques are developed within the individual to counter all
opponents. All their players have a good variation of services, mainly short
with all aspects of sidespin, backspin and topspin combinations.

Their best players, especially Stellan Bengtsson and Kjell Johansson,*
have very consistent backhand counter attacks that do not have excessive
spin but sufficient speed and excellent angles to create for the opponent
difficulties in obtaining forehand domination. This allows them time to
establish attacking domination with their backhand or forehand. They
play many strokes about three feet from the table edge, between the
backhand corner and centre of the table. They have excellent control of
blocking the loop and can vary the block with sidespin or topspin.

They usually prefer blocking if someone does get in with a loop, but they
are quite capable of either smashing the loop with their forehand or moving
back slightly and looping the loop, usually with more topspin than sidespin
(Figs. 1 and 2).

4 *Yugoslavia (1976 European Champions)*
The coaching system in this country is similar to Sweden in that they tend to
concentrate on coaching one style, but this style is different. In Dragutin
Surbek and Anton Stipancic the Yugoslavs have a pair of players as
outstanding as Bengtsson and Johansson of Sweden. Surbek tends to
dominate the table with forehand strokes whereas Stipancic uses his
backhand more often. Whenever possible, both of these players tend to

* Now non-playing captain of the Swedish National Table Tennis Teams.

Fig. 1   Stellan Bengtsson, Sweden, in action. Bengtsson was 1971 World Men's
Singles winner

Fig. 2   Kjell Johansson of Sweden, three times World Men's Doubles winner

Fig. 3 Dragutin Surbek, Yugoslavia. (1973 World Men's Singles semi-finalist, 1975 World Men's Doubles finalist.)

Fig. 4 Anton Stipancic, Yugoslavia. (1975 World Men's Singles finalist and 1975 World Men's Doubles finalist.)

impart topspin on the ball. They both have 'excellent touch' and if they cannot loop a service, they return the ball so that the opponent cannot play a devastating attacking stroke, then they get their loop drives into the rally. Surbek very rarely uses his backhand but concentrates on using his fitness to dominate with forehand loop drives. Stipancic is not as fit but he has wonderful control and imparts tremendous topspin and sidespin variation with both backhand and forehand. When receiving a loop drive they tend to stand further away from the table than the two Swedes and they play a loop return with both sidespin and topspin (Figs. 3 and 4).

5 *Hungary (1978 European Champions)*
After 1975 when Istvan Jonyer became the World Men's Singles Champion and the Men's Doubles Champion with his team-mate Gabor Gergely, the Hungarian National Teams were beset with injuries to their leading players. However, in the 1978 European Championships in Duisburg, West Germany, all the Hungarian players performed superbly and their men and women appeared in all seven finals.

Their men players won the team title, beating England 5–3 in the final, while in the Men's Singles event four of their players reached the quarter finals: Gabor Gergely, Istvan Jonyer, Tibor Kreisz and Tibor Klampar. The latter lost to Desmond Douglas (England) but the other three players reached the semi-finals and Gergely defeated Jonyer in the final. Gergely also won the Men's Doubles in partnership with Milan Orlowski (Czechoslovakia) and Klampar and Gabriella Szabo lost in the Mixed Doubles final.

The National team and the most promising players in the provinces of the country are coached in Budapest, under the guidance of their National Coach, Zoltan Berczik. The players are financially supported by the state and each player practises and performs physical training for approximately five hours per day.

The majority of their men players try to dominate their matches by using their forehand and backhand loop drives. Their forehand loop drives are very long strokes that impart tremendous amounts of topspin and sidespin upon the ball. Their backhand loop drives are also long strokes and they use this stroke more effectively than players from any other nation. If necessary they will allow the opponent to loop drive the ball and then they will loop the loop, a technique at which they excel.

Previous Hungarian teams have included some excellent defensive players. Kreisz, a promising yet not outstanding junior player in 1975, has now become one of the best defensive players in the world.

Women's teams

1 *The People's Republic of China (1977 World Champions)*
Like the men's team the women's team is very strong in its depth of table

Fig. 5 Zoya Rudnova of the U.S.S.R., using the penhold grip

tennis talent. They have counter attacking, loop driving and defensive players, all of whom are quite capable of beating most players in the world. The 1975 and 1977 World Championships produced a Chinese victory in the Women's Team Event and their leading player, Chang Li, twice reached the final of the Womens' Singles, before losing to Pak Yung Sun of North Korea on each occasion. There are still many doubts as to whether the finals in 1975 and in 1977 were 'friendship' games. As previously stated (page 109) Ke Hsin-Ai caused havoc with her awkward blocking game and the unusual rubber on her racket. Chu Hsiang Yun has an excellent defensive game and her variety of backspin is very difficult to detect on her backhand strokes.

2 *South Korea (2nd in 1977 World Championships)*
The South Korean women's team have a fine record. In 1973, they won the World Championships Team Event and they finished runners-up to China in 1975 and 1977.

Most of their attacking players use a penhold grip but they have good defensive players who use the shake hands grip. Ailesa Lee is their best attacking player but as well as an excellent 'up to the table' game she has the exceptional ability to topspin lob very well when playing well away from the table. Chung Hyun Sook has a fine defensive game and her superb fitness allows her to move gracefully about the table. The variation of spin on her defensive strokes often confuses her opponents and this results in their making errors or setting the ball up in such a position that she can use a forehand smash.

3 *Hungary (1978 European Champions)*
Like their men counterparts the top lady players have missed many of the

leading tournaments over the past few years because of injuries.

Judit Magos, Beatrix Kishazi and Gabriella Szabo easily won the European Team Championships in Duisburg. Magos beat Jill Hammersley (England) in the final of the Women's Singles and she lost in the finals of the Women's Doubles partnered by Szabo. These players have contrasting styles of play and none is similar to the Hungarian men. Magos uses an unorthodox penhold grip and like most penhold grip players she has a good combination of forehand strokes. Kishazi has an excellent defensive game and Szabo has a good counter attacking and loop drive game.

In the 1979 World Table Tennis Championships in Pyongyang, North Korea, the People's Republic of China retained the right to consider itself the leading nation in the world when their players captured four of the seven titles. In the Mixed Doubles and Women's Doubles Finals all the players were from the People's Republic of China; the only final in which they were not represented was in the Men's Doubles. The Chinese women players won all their events, but one of the major surprises of the championships was that their men failed to win the Men's Team Event or the Men's Singles. Seiji Ono, a left-handed attacking player, retained the Men's Singles title for Japan when he defeated Kuo Yao Hua of China, in an ill-fated final in which the latter was forced to retire with a torn hamstring. The Hungarian Men's Team, the 1978 European Champions, played superbly and probably surprised even themselves when they crushed the People's Republic of China 5–1 in the Men's Team Event final. This very impressive victory will no doubt create a great deal of interest for players, coaches and spectators alike as to what style of play will be the most effective in the future.

RESULTS OF THE 1979 WORLD TABLE TENNIS CHAMPIONSHIPS

MEN'S TEAM EVENT:	Hungary bt China 5–1		
WOMEN'S TEAM EVENT:	China bt North Korea 3–1		
MEN'S SINGLES:	Seiji Ono (Japan)	bt	Kuo Yao Hua (China) 25–23, 21–17, 18–21, 3–0 retired hurt
WOMEN'S SINGLES:	Ke Hsin Ai (China)	bt	Li Song Suk (North Korea) 21–18, 21–16, 21–19
MEN'S DOUBLES:	Dragutin Surbek and Anton Stipancic (Yugoslavia)	bt	Istvan Jonyer and Tibor Klampar (Hungary) 21–18, 22–20, 21–16
WOMEN'S DOUBLES:	Chang Li and Zhang Deying (China)	bt	Ge Xinai and Yan Guili (China) 21–13, 21–14, 21–16
MIXED DOUBLES:	Liang Ke Liang and Ge Xinai (China)	bt	Li Chen Shih and Yan Guili (China) 21–16, 21–16, 21–15

7 The Development of Physical Fitness to Assist Table Tennis Performance

It is now usually accepted that to perform creditably at table tennis a player has to be dedicated, have adequate motivation and undergo a system of fitness training that is based on scientific principles. The basic components of fitness are strength, cardio-respiratory endurance, local muscular endurance, power, speed, agility, mobility, flexibility and balance. These attributes may be to a certain extent inborn but they have to be developed in a systematic manner based on principles of training which have evolved through time. The criterion of skill combined with power is the most important aspect of fitness in which a table tennis player should excel but it is necessary to explain each component of fitness in some detail. Before dealing with the acquisition and the development of different physical qualities and the exercises which produce them, it is necessary to explain briefly how training improves physical fitness.

HOW THE BODY FUNCTIONS

In its many forms, training is the means by which we try to accustom the body to an improved standard of performance. Training improves the efficiency of the body's various physiological systems – muscular, respiratory, cardio-vascular, etc. – so that they are able to function efficiently at the higher standard demanded of them. To understand how training methods effect this improvement we must first look at how the body functions.

During table tennis, striped or voluntary muscles cause the actual body movements. These muscles consist of thousands of long, dark- and light-coloured fibres bound together in bundles enclosed in sheaths. These are attached to bones by tendons and white fibrous tissue. When the muscles contract they shorten and pull the bones, thus moving parts of the body. Muscles, like all working things, require energy materials. We obtain these from some of the food we eat, in the form of glycogen and metabolised fat. Some glycogen is kept in the muscles for immediate use but most is kept in the body's storehouse – the liver. When the body uses energy material, waste products are produced which, if left behind, would clog the muscles up. To break down these waste products the body uses oxygen, obtained from the air around us in another of the body's systems called the lungs. In fact, the lungs perform several functions: they obtain and supply air and they remove waste products such as carbon dioxide (CO_2), water and excess heat.

The body requires a transport system to deliver oxygen and glycogen to the muscles and to remove waste products. This function is performed by the blood, which contains plasma to deliver nutrients, and red cells to deliver oxygen and remove carbon dioxide. Waste materials are also removed by the blood. Such a transport system needs a network of 'roads' along which to travel. These come in the form of connected tubes called arteries, along which the blood delivers energy material and oxygen, and veins along which it removes waste products.

Since the transport system uses fluids, some form of pump is needed to force it along the arteries and veins. The body's pump is the heart which is actually two pumps connected together. It, too, is made of muscle fibres, but of a more complicated type than the voluntary muscles used in body movement. The heart collects the blood containing waste products from the muscles and pumps it to the lungs. There the waste products are removed and replaced by oxygen. The heart then collects the blood again, this time from the lungs, and pumps it back to the muscles. Some blood is also sent to the liver to collect more energy materials. In this way there is a continuous supply of energy material and of oxygen, and a continuous removal of waste products so that they do not clog the muscle.

THE DEVELOPMENT OF STAMINA

Definition

According to Vaughan Thomas, stamina is defined as the 'ability to withstand fatigue'[1]. For our purpose fatigue is anything which tends to cause a fall off in table tennis physical performance.

According to Randall, Waine and Hicklin it is important to differentiate between an 'endurance which is mainly local in character and that which is dependent upon the cardiovascular-respiratory system'[2]. Johnson, Updyke, Stolberg and Schaefer supply the following definitions[3].

Muscular endurance
'The capacity to persist in localised muscular effort.'

Circulo-respiratory endurance
The capacity of 'the individual to persist in strenuous tasks for periods of some length'.

Factors influencing endurance

Morehouse and Miller's[4] investigations showed the following:

THE DEVELOPMENT OF PHYSICAL FITNESS 119

1. *Strength*
If a high level of strength exists in a muscle group then a player should be able to increase his endurance in that particular muscle group.

2. *Fat*
If a player is overweight he is usually carrying too many fat deposits. This extra, unnecessary load has to be carried every time the player makes a movement. Extra energy has to be used to move this extra weight so it follows that excess fat becomes a limiting factor in endurance.

3. *Circulation*
The speed at which oxygen reaches various muscle groups in the body will depend upon the rate of circulation of the blood.

4. *Motivation*
When a player is in a state of fatigue and he is feeling discomfort and pain he must have enough will power to keep moving (going through the pain barrier).

5. *Skill*
A very good player usually has good neuro-muscular coordination. Therefore he is not expending energy on unnecessary muscle movements. Less skilful players will use up more oxygen for a similar movement or stroke.

6. *Distribution of energy*
A player should be able to work at his maximum capacity throughout the entire game.

7. *Pace*
A player should have a good recovery rate after exercise so that he can play well in every match of a particular tournament.

8. *Cheering*
Psychological factors such as cheering and encouragement can assist a player in giving his best in training or in a competition.

Principles of training
Some of the principles of training suggested by Doherty[5] include:

1. An endurance training programme should be developed that will improve physiological and mental qualities. The training should increase in a systematic manner.
2. In the early stages of a training programme long distance running should be performed to improve stamina.
3. Careful progression in the degree of intensity of each training session should be undertaken to improve stamina.

4. Specialised aspects of a training programme should be introduced when a basic fitness level has been achieved. Therefore, table tennis players should develop those muscles that are specifically needed for their own style of game after they have achieved a broad foundation of fitness.
5. Every training programme should be developed specifically for each individual. It is important to consider what will be the best type of training to suit a player's emotions and social surroundings.
6. A player should always be aware of whether his training programme is developing endurance or strength. An endurance programme will improve the development of blood capillaries whereas a strength programme is more concerned with the development of muscle fibres.
7. A correct training programme for a group of people can be motivationally beneficial.
8. When the table tennis season has begun, a player's training programme should be designed to maintain, rather than increase, his level of fitness.
9. Both general and specific fitness must be carefully planned throughout the whole year.
10. A training programme should be designed so that a player is well prepared for important tournaments.
11. A well scheduled programme should be designed so that a player does not become bored.
12. A simple programme can be an effective programme.

Methods of training for circulo-respiratory endurance

Long distance running
A good form of endurance training is long distance running at a steady speed. Depending on the player's existing fitness, the distance could vary from two to ten miles. Concentration should be kept on not varying the pace.

Interval training
The best training system demands maximum performance in the shortest time and with least effort. Interval training today for table tennis players is performed mainly from June for winter preparation and emphasis is on quality. It is restricted to the track and a definite schedule is adhered to; both runs and intervals are timed. An example is 300 yd × 'Y' with two minute intervals. De Vries is of the opinion that 'Improvement in endurance factors is brought about not so much by increasing the total work as by decreasing the rest intervals'[6]. One disadvantage of interval training is the possibility of boredom. Another is that if one cuts down on the rest period too much then the actual running may not be so beneficial. Many athletes agree that interval training gives endurance but not all can decide whether long rests and long runs or brief rests and fast short runs are the more advantageous.

Fartlek

Another type of training popular for players is called *fartlek*, developed in Sweden. The Swedish National Team use it often during the summer months. It follows the principles of speed and endurance; training must be suited to the individual. It started well in Sweden because it appealed to the people and the terrain of their countryside. It involves running amongst forests and soft surfaces around lakes at varying tempos, over various distances, up and down hills, at different running speeds. An example could be: five minutes' easy running, followed by steady hard running for one mile, then five minutes' fast walking, jogging, uphill running, one hundred and fifty yards of repetitions and finally running at a fast pace for one to three minutes.

Really the runner progresses without the pressures of coaches and stopwatch, track training, boredom or staleness which causes body and mind fatigue. The important thing to remember is not just to plod along; and in the months of May and June it should be combined with other training methods. It is better done for a time than for a distance, and progress can be measured by length of run within the set time. Many people believe in training away from the track, by running on sand dunes or heavy wet soil surfaces. The limitations of *fartlek* are that there is little opportunity for pace work, and speed work is limited when attempted on a soft surface.

Circuit training

A form of progressive resistance training for physical fitness is circuit training. It allows individual training with limited supervision and also has a satisfying appeal in that it is simple and one can observe self-improvement. It aids the development of a high level of functional ability based on mobility, speed, strength and endurance. It has been stated that circuit training 'aims at progressive development of muscular and circulatory-respiratory fitness'[7]. It also conditions the muscles and coordinates the actions of muscle groups, as well as mobilising the movements of levers. The tissue viscosity of muscles and the supply of blood to the muscle are also improved. With this form of training a player will obtain a better work rate, in muscle groups that are used in performing a particular stroke. The continuous activity of these muscle groups in training and in matches will also assist circulo-respiratory endurance.

Circuit training contributes to progressive increase in work rate, and is simple enough for all. It is good for the body because it is performed at a high work rate with small rest periods so continuous demands are made on the heart and lungs. Time elements can be initiated and sub-maximal limits. Muscle groups should be exercised in turn, i.e. arms, legs, trunk etc.

A circuit can be devised simply by setting a number of exercises. Players are made to perform each exercise correctly, then see how many of each they can do in a minute allowing rests between each exercise of about one minute. The number of repetitions for each exercise is halved and this number will be performed in the next session so that each exercise is performed in turn, three times. The total time is taken and in future weeks, this time has to be improved by as much as possible. The improvement obtained will depend on the initial fitness, and in really fit people their fixed dosage may be two thirds of their maximal.

There is the psychological advantage that weaker players gain satisfaction whilst working independently at their own rate, and are quite happy to mix with the better ones. They are free from directions and yet many people can work in a group, although tested individually. All-round fitness is essential before high level skill is applied in table tennis, so circuit training is excellent. Excellence should be integrated with physiological efficiency and physical power.

Walking
Walking over a long distance with a pack on the back is also very useful for developing endurance. The pack acts as an extra weight which the body is not used to carrying and which causes resistance to movement. This can be a very aesthetic way of training as the scenery on carefully chosen walks can be delightful. The addition of a few slopes or hills will again add to the aesthetic pleasure, but more important it will assist in adding resistance to the musculature of the body.

Pressure training on the table
(See advanced training programme, pages 84–100)

Methods of training for muscular endurance
As mentioned previously this is concerned with more specific training on certain areas of the body. The table tennis player needs endurance in most areas of the body.

Weight training
A good way of training is by the use of weights. Light weights should be used in relation to body strength for each particular area, and training should consist of many repetitions of each exercise. Before trying this type of training make sure that you are properly instructed in the lifting and lowering of the weights and the safety precautions. Any good weight training book will supply this information and also numerous exercises for any part of the human body. Another essential point to remember, as in circuit training, is to arrange the exercises so that each group of muscles is exercised in turn, thus avoiding consecutive exercises testing the same set of muscles. This cycle of exercises must allow for sufficient rest periods for each group of muscles. A very simple type of endurance exercise is set out in Appendix A. Adjustments may have to be made in weights to allow for the condition of the individual.

Circuit training
As for cardiovascular development, this type of training is ideal for developing muscular endurance in the required areas of the body. Many sets of exercises can be done with or without equipment. A circuit for arm, leg and abdominal regions for good strong men players could include:

STAR JUMPS (See Chapter 8, Fig. 11) Make sure the hands touch the ground between the legs. Full upright extension of the body is gained when travelling upwards. Up and down counts as one.

SIT UPS (see Chapter 8, Fig. 12) The knees need not be flat on the floor and one need only rise to 90°. Keep hands locked behind the head. Up and down counts as one.

PRESS UPS (see Chapter 8, Fig. 13) Ensure that the buttocks are in line with the shoulders and feet. Lower the body so that the elbow joints are flexed at 90°. Up and down counts as one.

KNEE JUMPS (see Chapter 8, Fig. 14) Raise both legs together so knees reach waist height. Keep upright. Up and down counts as one.

'V' ARCHES (see Chapter 8, Fig. 15) The legs are raised off the ground in line with the upper body so a 'V' shape is formed. Legs need not necessarily be straight. The head comes as close to the legs as possible. Up and down counts as one.

PLUTO SNIFFS (see Chapter 8, Fig. 16) Legs should remain apart and relatively straight. The upper body moves by arm movements so that the head travels in a forward direction first and eventually through an anti-clockwise circle (if looking from the left). The nose should almost touch the ground surface from in front of the hands to behind them. Once around counts as one.

Interval running
Concentration should be on high speeds with little recovery time. This will be really good for leg musculature endurance. An example could be 180 yd × 10 with forty seconds rest between sprints. Each 180 yd should be covered in less than 30 seconds.

Fartlek or beach runs
Once again concentration should be more on the speed aspect, with shorter intervals of rest.

Uphill running
As before in fast interval forms, i.e. 50 yd × 15 with 40 second rest periods.

THE DEVELOPMENT OF STRENGTH

The maximal strength that a skeletal muscle possesses can be calculated by the maximal force it exerts in one contraction. The strength of the muscle will be affected by the length of the muscle, the angle of its insertion to a bone and its muscular cross section. Although muscles may have a similar circumference it does not necessarily follow that they are equal in strength. Various tests by exercise physiologists [8, 9] have determined that individuals with large skeletal muscles score well in strength tests and that strength is an important factor in sports performance.

Factors influencing strength

Muscle circumference
The force with which a muscle can contract will depend upon the amount of fat tissue in the muscle. Therefore, a fat flabby muscle will affect its contractile force.

Physique
'The total strength that a player can develop will be restricted by his body structure.'[10]

Calibre of muscle
The strength of contraction of a skeletal muscle will depend on the amount of training that particular muscle has received. The contractile force of different muscle groups will vary, and the relative strengths of an individual's muscle groups will be influenced by the environment in which he lives and his daily schedule.

Muscle inervation
The force with which a muscle can contract will depend upon the number and size of the fibres that are brought into use. However, this is dependent upon the efficiency of the nervous system.

Muscle insertion
When a player plays a stroke in table tennis, the contractile force applied to the ball and the speed of movement will depend upon the number of muscles involved in the joint action and the length of the bone levers. The mechanical power that a joint can produce will be increased if the muscle is inserted further away from the joint. 'Most muscles have very short force arms in the leverage system in which they work. A slight change (even $\frac{1}{4}$ in.) in the insertion might make a significant difference to the force that the muscle can exert.'[11]

Energy stores
If a player does not eat the correct amount and type of food, the quality and quantity of fuel may affect muscular contraction.

Age and sex

Muscular strength increases as the growth in the size of a muscle increases during childhood. A player usually reaches his maximum strength in his mid-twenties,[12] but he can maintain a similar level of strength if he has a regular training programme. Differences in strength exist between the sexes and tests have shown that the average grip strength of women is 62 per cent that of men.[13]

Improving strength

Different forms of exercise have different effects in developing muscle strength. Much will depend upon the particular exercise and the work rate. In the light of available scientific information:

1 An exercise programme prepared to increase strength should be evaluated on the amount of work performed in a time-period and not the total amount of work done.
2 Strenuous exercises which can work a muscle to its limit will stimulate that muscle to develop in strength.
3 If a player can repeatedly lift a light load then the gain in strength will be miminal.
4 For improvement to be attained the amount of training must be greater than the normal daily stress requirements upon the body.

Specificity in training

Although the value of strength is no longer debated, this does not necessarily imply that we should go to the other extreme and develop massive strength only. Our first concern should be to ensure an all-round strengthening of the body. Selection of activities for strengthening work should be based on such criteria as:

1 Analysis of the movement involved in the particular stroke, in terms of type, speed, direction, etc.
2 Groups of muscles involved in these movements.
3 Sequence of movements, etc.

Special exercises designed to approximate as closely as possible to the same pattern and rate of movement, or part of the movement, should be performed, as this will bring into play the specific groups of muscles required for the particular event.

In respect of strength training for any particular sport, like table tennis, it is important to be able to know:

1 The degree of strength required by the individual for championship performance. ·
2 The kind of strength required.
3 The time to be devoted to strength development.
4 The most effective method to be employed.

METHODS OF TRAINING FOR STRENGTH

Strength is essential in table tennis players, because it assists greatly in power. Certain muscles of the body need to be very strong so as to enable the weight of the body to be transported as effectively as possible. The thighs and the calf muscles need to be strong to move the body frame. The abdominals are an important factor in maintaining movement so as to ensure a good continuation in the build up, when playing a stroke. The racket arm is also very important, as it must travel as quickly and effectively as possible. This is not to say the trunk region is not important. One must remember that in all sports and not just table tennis, force must travel through all areas of the body in a fluent manner so as to give maximum effect. If a certain muscle is weak and it is in a pathway of the direction of force it will not assist in the increase of force during its transference to the ball.

Weight training

An excellent way of developing strength is by weight training and with heavy weights and low repetitions. For each group of muscles involved one finds out one's maximum lift, then does X number of lifts at Y lb below this weight. Then as the weight increases the number of repetitions will drop. Once a player has achieved two lifts at maximum weight, 5 lb are added and a new maximum may be achieved. Strength training can also be developed with springs if no weights are available. Examples of weight training for strength can include:

Half squats	180 lb × 5	Two-arm curl	50 lb × 5
	190 lb × 4		60 lb × 4
	200 lb × 3		70 lb × 2
	210 lb × 2		80 lb × 1
	220 lb × 1		

Any good weight training book will give many examples of different lifts, poundages and rest periods.[14]

It is very important for a table tennis player to have strength and flexibility in his wrist, so that quick powerful movements can be made (especially for serving). Good exercises can be performed with dumb-bells for adduction, abduction, extension and flexion of the wrist joint.

Isometrics

Professor E. A. Muller and Dr Hettinger of the Max Planck Institute, Dortmund, when investigating isometrics, developed a new type of strength training.[15] They reported that those people who did not have much time could achieve maximum training effect with only 40 to 50 per cent of application. The contractions were against a maximum load and held for a short duration. The muscle appears to be in a static state and may only be strengthened at the position at which the exercise occurs. This type of training seems to have little effect on dynamic strength or cardio-respiratory endurance.

One example of this type of training is arm and shoulder strengthening by pressing the hands together. The grip can be strengthened by trying to squeeze a hockey ball. The abdominals can be improved by attempting to lift wall bars with the feet. A good survey on isometric exercises can be found in the book *Pure and Applied Gymnastics* by Munrow.[16]

Circuit Training
One can plan a training programme to emphasise the development of strength. One must concentrate on performing exercises where many repetitions are difficult and a maximum of eight should not be exceeded.

Examples can include weight lifting at stages in the circuit.

1 *Rope Climbs*
2 *Sit-ups* on an inclined bench. (Weights can be added to the hands to increase the resistance.)
3 *Half squats* with a weight that allows about six repetitions at the commencement of the course.
4 *Pull-ups* (Weights can be tied to the waist to increase resistance.)
5 *Leg raising* with weighted shoes heavy enough to make six the maximum.
6 *Extending legs* against leg pressing machine where only six counts are possible.

Each time the exercise is performed it should include as many repetitions as possible. If a count reaches eight, then the task should be made more difficult by increasing the resistance.

DEVELOPMENT OF POWER AND SPEED

Power
Mechanically, power is the rate of doing work. Power = Force × Velocity = Force × Distance/Time. It is speed and strength combined to develop fast explosive movements. Morgan and Adamson summarise in the statement that 'power shows itself in the ability to propel one's own body or some other object rapidly through space'.[17] A weight that is light in comparison to a muscle's maximum capacity can be moved faster than a weight that is almost the same.

Speed
While acknowledging the role of efficient neuro-muscular coordination, Hill[18] supports the theory that the speed of muscular contraction is an inherited ability. From the above statements one can easily imagine the importance of speed and power in making a good table tennis player.

THE DEVELOPMENT OF POWER AND SPEED

Power
Weight training
This time slightly heavier than medium weights are used and repetitions are performed explosively but with relatively long recoveries.

Example (this will depend on the player's condition):

Two-handed curls   50 lb × 8; 3 sets; 1 minute's rest
Half squats   150 lb × 8; 3 sets; 1 minute's rest
Sit ups   10 lb × 8; 3 sets; 1 minute's rest

Sprints All forms of sprinting are excellent power builders.

Speed
Mobility exercises; acceleration runs; short test sprints; downhill runs; sprint starts.

DEVELOPMENT OF FLEXIBILITY

Two definitions of flexibility (Cureton[19])
1 'Flexibility means the capacity to bend, or to be flexed or extended without breaking; to be pliant, not stiff or brittle. Similar words are limber, lithe and supple.'
2 'Capable of being bent, admitting to change in figure without breaking, yielding to pressure, pliable, capable of modification or adaption.'

Range of movements
The range of movements will depend on the particular joints and include

Fig. 1

a *Flexion*   **b** *Hyperextension*   **c** *Abduction*

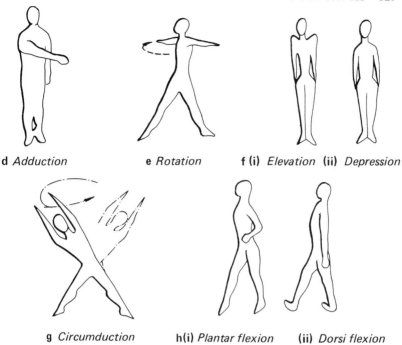

d *Adduction*   e *Rotation*   f (i) *Elevation* (ii) *Depression*

g *Circumduction*   h(i) *Plantar flexion*   (ii) *Dorsi flexion*

i *Supination*
Hands down by the side the palms
facing the front.

j *Pronation*
Hands down by the side but palms
face backwards.

The acceleration of movement of a joint will depend on certain muscles and the state of the muscle could well influence the degree of flexibility in the joint. Certain muscles act as 'fixators'. This means they fix a particular base upon which movements of other muscles may be made. The bones and muscles can be joined by collagenous fibres (for strength), elastic fibres (for elasticity), reticular fibres (for framework of tissues), ligaments (mainly for strengthening function) and cartilages (whose function is to resist compression and tension). Their potential can vary the amount of flexibility.

Other factors involved in flexibility include:

PHYSIQUE: Several types of measurement would differ depending upon the size of body segments.

AGE: Change of metabolism. Changing make up of connective tissues. Slowing up of regenerative and repair mechanisms.

ENVIRONMENT: Where one works (e.g. confined-space work by miners or similar occupations).

EXERCISE: Effects of training and sports as one ages.

INJURY: Relative inelasticity of scar tissue. Orthopaedic injury. Adhesion in uninjured limbs.

It is fairly obvious that both ligamentous structure and muscle contraction and relaxation are of importance and that it is essential that table tennis players have good flexibility so as to assist movement and control. Tests can be performed as described in Chapter 8, Tests and Measurements. Exercises for flexibility and mobility can be fitted ideally into warm-up exercises or used as a separate programme. They can be isotonic or isometric in nature. Testing has proved that both can increase flexibility and are equally effective. (See Appendix B)

Isotonic pre-match warm-up
There are many exercises that can be performed for various movements of different joints. Here are just a few examples:

1 *Fingers*
Manipulation at all possible angles (20 seconds).

2 *Wrists*
a) ABDUCTION AND ADDUCTION OR RADIAL FLEXION AND ULNAR FLEXION: Join the palms of the hands together so that the fingers are pointing away from the body and the elbows are flexed at 90°. Keeping the palms together, turn the fingers towards the chin so as to face in the direction of the chest. Return the fingers to the starting position (10 times slow, 10 times fast).

b) EXTENSION: With the elbows flexed at 90° and the hands in a pronated position bring the backs of the hands towards the forearms and then return to the starting position (10 times slow, 10 times fast).

c) FLEXION: Try to touch the front of the forearm with the fingers of the same hand (10 times slow, 10 times fast).

3 *Elbow joints*
Flex the elbows so that the fingers touch the shoulders and return to a supine position by the sides of the body (10 times slow, 10 times fast).

4 *Radio-ulnar joints*
Turn the hands from a pronated to a supinated position (10 times slow, 10 times fast).

5 *Shoulder girdle*
a) ADDUCTION AND ABDUCTION: Hold the right shoulder with the left hand and the left shoulder with the right hand so the arms are crossing in front of the body. Exert a little pressure, then keeping the elbows at the

same height, throw out the arms to the sides (10 times slow, 10 times fast).

b) ELEVATION AND DEPRESSION: Try to reach as far down the sides of the legs as possible but with the trunk not moving forward or laterally. Then lift the shoulders as high as possible (10 times slow, 10 times fast).

c) UPWARD AND DOWNWARD ROTATION: The finger tips of each hand meet just under the chin and the elbows are at shoulder height. The shoulder girdle then moves by the elbows making circular movements while the fingers stay in the same position (10 times slow, 10 times fast, in clockwise and anti-clockwise directions).

6 *Shoulder joint*
a) FLEXION, EXTENSION AND HYPEREXTENSION: Start by placing the arms straight out in front of the body, shoulder-width apart, then commence movement by coming downwards and continue so that they go as far behind you as possible (10 times slow, 10 times fast).

b) ABDUCTION AND ADDUCTION: The arms are elevated out to the side of the body and then returned (10 times slow, 10 times fast).

c) INWARD AND OUTWARD ROTATION: This can be performed by placing the arms out to the side at shoulder height, with the palms of the hands in a mid-prone position. When all the arm turns forward this is known as inward rotation and when it turns backwards it is known as outward rotation (10 times slow, 10 times fast, in clockwise and anti-clockwise directions).

d) CIRCUMDUCTION: Exercises are performed by moving the extended arm in a circular pattern about the joint. This should be done so the arm passes close to the head and body (10 times slow, 10 times fast in clockwise and anti-clockwise directions).

e) HORIZONTAL ABDUCTION AND ADDUCTION: These movements are very necessary as they are often used in table tennis strokes. Each arm should be exercised in turn by starting in a position where the elbow is flexed and at shoulder height. Keeping the fingers at chin height, the elbow is brought as far forward and inward as possible then returned to a point as far back as possible. All the time the elbow is kept at shoulder height.

7 *Movements in the spinal column*
a) In the first and second cervical vertebrae, i.e. 'the atlas and axis', a combination of extension, flexion, lateral and rotary movements can

occur. Good exercises for mobility include:

head forward and backwards; head side to side; rotation in clockwise direction and rotation in an anti-clockwise direction. Each should be done 10 times slowly and 10 times fast.

b) FLEXION IN OTHER VERTEBRAE: Mostly free in the lumbar area. A simple exercise includes bending forward, with the feet astride, and touching either the tops of the socks, ankles or toes depending upon one's capabilities. Gradual improvement can occur. The legs should remain as straight as possible (10 times slow, 10 times fast).

c) EXTENSION IN OTHER VERTEBRAE: This is possible in all vertebrae but hyperextension is more marked in the lumbar region and lower two thoracic segments. This exercise can be combined with the flexion exercise if on returning from touching the toes the fingers stretch up and backwards behind the head as far as possible while the feet are kept firmly on the ground in the astride position.

d) LATERAL FLEXION: This is possible at all levels, but is most free at the junction of the thoracic and lumbar regions. A simple exercise is that of touching as far as possible down the side of each leg alternately. Both feet are kept firmly on the ground (10 times slow, 10 times fast).

e) ROTATION: Rotation is more free in the upper part of the spine. Right rotation occurs when the pelvis is fixed and the head and shoulders turn to the right. However, right rotation also occurs if the upper body is fixed as in 'hanging' from a beam and the pelvis is turned to the left. Really in all rotary movements lateral flexion occurs and vice-versa. Exercises can include:

    i) Twisting the body so the right hand goes behind the body and touches the rear of the left knee and after returning to the upright position the left hand then touches the rear of the right knee (10 times slow, 10 times fast).

    ii) Keeping the elbows out at shoulder height and the hands together, the twisting action occurs so that the right elbow extends as far clockwise as possible, then the left elbow twists as far anti-clockwise as possible (10 times slow, 10 times fast).

8 *Hip Joint*

a) FLEXION: A good exercise is to try and kick the hand which is outstretched at about chest height in front of you (10 times slow, 10 times fast).

b) EXTENSION: This exercise can be done as a continuation of the flexion exercise by allowing the leg to swing as far down and back as possible (10 times slow, 10 times fast).

c) ABDUCTION: A good exercise is to stand with the left shoulder touching the wall and swing the right leg out to the side as far as possible. Then change around and swing the left leg (10 times slow, 10 times fast, each leg).

d) ADDUCTION: It is easier to adduct if the other leg is slightly forward or back, so a good exercise is to swing the right leg across the front of the left leg and then return and swing to the back of the left leg. The left leg can be adducted by reversing the procedure (10 times slow, 10 times fast, each leg).

e) CIRCUMDUCTION: This is a combination of flexion, extension, abduction and adduction. Balance is maintained on one foot while the other foot describes a conical shape off the ground. The circumference of the circle described by the toes is gradually increased (10 times clockwise, 10 times anti-clockwise, each leg in turn).

f) ROTATION: Inward rotation is when the toes move towards the centre of the body. Outward rotation is when they move away.
Take the foot off the ground and turn the toes as far as possible to each side. Ensure the leg is straight (10 times each way for each leg).

9 *Knee joint*
a) FLEXION AND EXTENSION: Numerous exercises can assist in producing flexibility. The essential thing is to try and use up all the 135° range of flexion which is usually achieved. There are simple exercises like bringing the heel up to the thigh, then propelling the foot as if kicking a football as in a rugby punt (10 times slow, 10 times fast, each leg).

b) INWARD AND OUTWARD ROTATION: This can be performed only if the leg is in a flexed position. It is a very essential movement for table tennis, as it assists in pivoting when changing direction to play a stroke. A good exercise is to stand in the forehand attacking ready stance position and practice pivoting to play a backhand and then a forehand.

10 *The ankle joint and joints in the foot*
a) DORSIFLEXION AND PLANTAR FLEXION OF THE FOOT: This can be done by raising one foot at a time off the ground and extending as far down as possible with the toes (plantar flexion) and then bringing them up to try and touch the anterior surface of the leg (dorsiflexion). Dorsal and plantar flexion takes place only in the ankle joint and slightly in the tarsal joint (10 times slow, 10 times fast, each foot).

b) EVERSION AND INVERSION: Eversion is when the foot is turned out-wards. It takes place only in the tarsal joints. Inversion is when the foot is turned inwards and also takes place only in the tarsal joints. A simple but effective exercise is balancing on the heels and moving the toes to an inward 'pigeon' position, then as far out as possible (10 times slow, 10 times fast, each direction). There are, of course, numerous different exercises which could be used. Only a few have been mentioned here, to give a simple guide.

Isometric pre-match warm-up

This is done as a form of yoga activity and as previously stated the muscles are in a static state, but there is an effect on the particular joints to improve flexibility. Without going into great detail of every joint, here are some examples:[20]

> *Upper trunk stretcher* (Figs. 2a and 2b)
> a) Pelvis on floor, extend arms.
> b) Extend upper body.
>
> *Lower trunk stretcher* (Figs. 3a and 3b)
> a) Grasp ankles from behind and pull.
> b) Hold head up.
>
> *Lower back stretcher* (Figs. 4a and 4b)
> a) Legs extended, toes pointed.
> b) Grasp outer edge of feet and pull head downwards.
>
> *Upper back stretcher* (Figs. 5a and 5b)
> a) Raise legs up and over the head.
> b) Rest extended toes on the floor.
> c) Leave hands and arms flat on the floor.

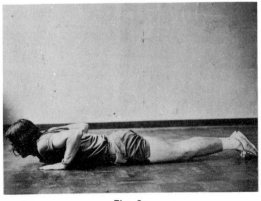

Fig. 2a

Fig. 2b

Fig. 3a

Fig. 3b

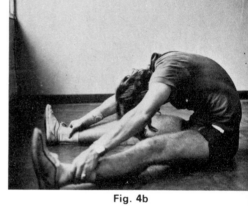

Fig. 4a

Fig. 4b

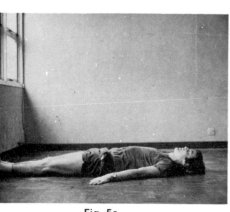

Fig. 5a

Fig. 5b

Gastrocnemius stretcher (Fig. 6)
a) Feet 3 ft to 4 ft from wall.
b) Body upright.
c) Keep feet parallel and flat on the floor.

Toe pointer (Figs. 7a–c)
a) Sit on feet, toes and ankles stretched backwards.
b) Raise knees from the floor.
c) Balance weight on both hands on the floor just behind the hips.

Shoulder stretcher (Figs. 8a and 8b)
a) Bring right hand from upper back.
b) Left hand from below.
c) Repeat from other side.

Fig. 6

Fig. 7a

Fig. 7b

Fig. 7c

Fig. 8a

Fig. 8b

These positions should be held for 15 to 20 seconds and by the eighth session one should be able to hold certain positions for up to one minute.

A player rarely notices how many different movements he actually performs during the course of a match. Many times, so many different joints of the body are performing actions in certain ways. Often wrong joint actions are occurring and it is the responsibility of the coach to draw attention to these bad joint action habits and instill the correct movements. To explain all the joint movements made and how they are made when a player plays a particular stroke needs a book in itself, but just as an example let us look at a few movements in a simple backhand counter-attacking stroke.

There is extension of the toes, plantar flexion in the ankle joint and slight inversion of the feet. The knees are flexed and then extended. There is a degree of right rotation in the hip joint and spinal column. Flexion in the shoulder girdle precedes a flexion, abduction and rotation in the shoulder joint. There is extension of the elbow joint. The wrist may be abducted, adducted, flexed or extended. For all these joint actions there may be as many as twelve different muscles coordinating to produce a certain action. It is enough to say here that the coach should have sufficient knowledge to know where to look and how to correct without needing to become a kinesiologist.

The physiological effects of training

Circulatory system
1 There is an increase in the number of latent capillaries. The numerical

increase will depend upon the severity of the training.[21] More blood will become available to the working tissues and local muscular endurance will increase.

2 There is usually a decrease in the resting heart rate after an endurance training programme. Thus, there is an increase in the stroke volume of the heart and this results in a more efficient heart rate.

3 With the progression of an exercise programme the heart is capable of returning to a lower heart rate per minute in a certain period of time. This shows an improvement in the efficiency of the circulatory system.

4 There is a 10 to 19 per cent increase in blood volume after a nine-week training programme.[22] There is an increase in red blood cells so the blood has a greater oxygen-carrying capacity and the body can perform more work.

5 Due to an increase in the size of the capillaries there is an increase in the amount of oxygen that can be collected by the blood in the lungs. Similarly, there is a greater quantity of oxygen that can be distributed to the working tissues.

6 Cardiac output is increased with training so the amount of blood and oxygen that can be transported to the tissues per minute is increased.

7 During exercise lactic acid is produced. The amount of this lactic acid, which must be moved from muscle tissue, is increased because there are more capillaries, more blood and therefore oxygen. The lactic acid is oxidised to carbon dioxide and water.

8 Because of training, it is possible to have a more efficient blood distribution to various parts of the body. In certain instances it may be more important to increase the supply of blood and oxygen to other parts of the body instead of the working muscles. With a trained athlete, for the same cardiac output, a greater proportion of blood can be utilised by other organs of the body. Training improves playing in hot temperatures because since less blood is required by the muscles, more blood can become available for the regulation of body temperature.

Muscular system

1 When a muscle contracts, a certain number of muscle fibres operate. Training will increase the number of muscle fibres that are capable of contracting, by bringing into use motor units not previously used. An increase in the number of fibres activated will contribute to an increase in strength.

2 The circumference of the muscle fibres will increase.[23] This hypertrophy occurs partly because of an increase in phosphocreatine (a compound of creatine and phosphoric acid that is used as an energy source in muscle contraction) and glycogen.

3 The thickness of the connective tissue increases within and around the muscles that were trained.[24]

4 The number of operational capillaries in the muscle tissue increases.[25] A

more efficient transportation system to and from the muscle is established. Oxygen and nutrients are capable of reaching the muscle in greater quantities and there is an improved rate of removal of lactic acid, carbon dioxide and water.

5 Training for specific tasks definitely increases muscular efficiency,[26] but a great deal of uncertainty exists as to whether this improvement is due to neuromotor patterns, circulo-respiratory changes or other causes. Further research is necessary before final conclusions can be established regarding the development of muscular power and endurance through training.

Respiratory system

1 After a training programme lasting a minimum of four weeks there are advantageous changes in the respiratory system of an individual. Physiological changes due to training include a larger oxygen consumption and a reduced carbon dioxide production. Therefore, there is a reduced rate of pulmonary ventilation so there is a reduction in the amount of work involved in breathing. The respiratory muscles increase their efficiency.

2 With the progression of a training programme, minute volume changes become apparent.[27] Ventilation becomes slower and deeper and the respiratory rate can drop considerably.

REFERENCES
 1 Thomas, V. (1970). *Science and sport*, p. 83. Faber: London.
 2 Randall, M., Waine, W. K. and Hicklin, M. J. (1967). *Objectives of the physical education lesson*. Bell and Hyman: London.
 3 Johnson, P. B., Updyke, W. F., Stolberg, D. C., Schaefer, M. (1966). *Physical education: A problem solving approach to health and fitness*, pp. 21–3. Holt, Rinehart and Winston, Inc.: New York.
 4 Morehouse, L. E. and Miller, A. T. Jr. (1976). *Physiology of exercise*, pp. 148–150, 152. Mosby: St. Louis.*
 5 Doherty, J. K. *Principles of training for endurance*.
 6 De Vries, H. (1970). *Physiology of exercise for physical education and athletics*, p. 219. Staples Press: London.*
 7 Morgan, R. E. and Adamson, G. T. (1965). *Circuit Training*, p. 13. Bell: London.*
 8 Clark, D. H. and Peterson, K. H. (1961). *Contrast of maturational structural and strength characteristics of athletes 10 to 15 years ago*, pp. 32–163. American Association for Health, Physical Education and Recreation.
 9 Whittle, H. D. (1956). 'Effects of elementary school physical education upon some aspects of physical, motor and personality development of boys twelve years of age.' Ph.D. Dissertation, University of Oregon, Eugene.
10 Sheldon, W. (1940). *The Varieties of Human Physique*. Harper: New York.
11 Hettinger, T. (1961). *Physiology of Strength*. Thomas: Illinois.*
12 Fisher, M. Bruce, and Birren, J. E. (1947), 'Age and strength.' *J. Appl. Physiology* **31**, 490–7.
13 Schmidt, Reynold T. and Toews, J. V. (1970). 'Grip strength as measured by the Jamar dynamometer.' *Arch. Phys. Med.* **51**, 321–7.

14 Hooks, G. (1974). *Weight Training in Athletics and Physical Education.* Prentice Hall: New Jersey.
15 Muller, E. G. and Hettinger, T. (1953). 'Muskelleistung and muskel training.' *Arbeitphysiologie* **15**, 111–26.
16 Munrow, A. D. (1963). *Pure and Applied Gymnastics.* Arnold: London.
17 Morgan, R. E. and Adamson, G. T. (1965). *Circuit training*, p. 18. Bell: London.
18 Hill, A. V. (1951). 'The mechanics of voluntary muscle.' *The Lancet* **261**, 947–51.
19 Cureton, T. K. (1941). 'Flexibility as an aspect of physical fitness.' *Research quarterly* **12**, 381–90.
20 A. De Vries, H. (1970). *Physiology of Exercise for Physical Education and Athletics*, p. 366. Staples Press: London.
21 O'Connor, F. and Sills, F. D. (1956). 'Heavy resistance exercise for basketball players.' *Athletics Journal* **39**, 6.
22 Kjellberg, S. R., Rudhe, V. and Sjostrand, T. (1949), 'Increase in the amount of haemoglobin and blood volume in connection with physical training.' *Acta. Physiological Scandinavica* **19**, 146–51.
23 Steinhaus, A. H. (1963). *Toward an Understanding of Health and Physical Education*, pp. 90, 93, 181. Brown.*
24 Ingelmark, B. E. (1957). 'Morphophysiological aspects of gymnastic exercises.' *Bulletin de la Fédération Internationale d'Education Physique* **27**, 37.
25 A. De Vries, H. (1970). *Physiology of Exercise for Physical Education and Athletes*, p. 293. Staples Press: London.
26 Johnson, P. B., Updyke, W. F. and Henry, W. (1965). 'Effect of regular exercise on diurnal variation in submaximal metabolism.' Paper presented at National Aapher Meeting.
27 Knehr, C. A., Dill, D. B. and Newfeld, W. (1942). 'Training and its effects in man at rest and work.' *Am. J. Physiol* **136**, 148.

* Recommended reading.

8 Tests and Measurements to Assess the Basic Fitness of Table Tennis Players

Physical and mental skills can be inherited and each individual is different. So a coach must realise what a player is capable of and then select a suitable programme of training. Tests and measurements can deal with immediate objectives and the progress of individuals towards certain goals. When one evaluates, one is judging the amount of change in a player in a period of time. Although good physical and mental development will greatly assist the learning situation in table tennis it will not necessarily produce a great champion. The champion must practise 'hard on the table as well as off'. For a table tennis player to function efficiently he must have organic and hereditary health, neuro-muscular coordination, strength and stability, emotional stability, social conscience, insight, attitudes, valued skills and morals.

When training players it is essential to measure all aspects of relevant fitness; find out the individual's weaknesses and then correct them. Before doing this, however, one must know exactly what type of fitness one wants to achieve. If a player can see himself improving physically it is a great psychological boost, and if he is training with his friends it can develop sound relationships and understanding of each other. When a coach is testing players he should make sure the tests are reliable, objective and valid. The norms he uses should have been delineated from a large random sample of subjects.

STRENGTH TESTS

When testing strength in a table tennis player it is important for the player to know why he is being tested. Many physiologists have shown that strength in an individual correlates with good performance in skills of a physical nature and that it is a big contribution towards total fitness. If a player is lacking in strength in relation to his size and weight, fatigue is more likely to occur and the peak of performance will be reduced. If one has good muscular development the body has every chance of functioning well and the development of new skills will be made easier. If one is feeling ill or is in a state of stress it is likely that strength will be affected.

To find a player's strength a good test is the *Physical Fitness Strength Index Test*. Over the past few years this test has had a reliability of 0·94.[1] It is essential that the player is well warmed up before each activity and one should always allow him a practice to make sure he is performing the activity correctly. Always mark down the readings at the earliest opportunity and check that the player has not suffered any injury.

The first test is for *lung capacity*, and uses a wet spirometer. One should exhale slowly into the apparatus after deep inspiration. To ensure maximum exhalation the player should bend forward. After each player has used the equipment the mouthpiece should be washed in diluted disinfectant. The reading one is interested in, is the amount of air exhaled after a single breath.

The second and third tests are for *right hand and left hand gripping strength*. For this test a manuometer should be used and the hand and arm should be abducted from the side of the body. Each hand is flexed in turn and the reading is taken on the manuometer to the nearest pound.

The fourth test is for *back-lift strength* and a back and leg dynomometer is used and in the fifth test for *leg strength*, the same apparatus is used. Once again, in each test the reading is recorded to the nearest pound.

The sixth test is the *pull up* on the beams, using an overgrasp grip. If the pull up does not include a complete lowering and raising of the chin above the beam only half a count is awarded. This test is combined with the seventh test which is the *dip* to ascertain arm strength. This latter exercise should be performed on parallel bars and the subject should jump to a support position with the arms straight. If he can lower the arm into a right-angled elbow position and push up again without his feet touching the floor, this will count as one repetition. If incorrect, half counts are awarded. The calculation of arm strength index is:

$$\left[\left(\begin{array}{c}\text{Number of}\\\text{pull ups}\end{array}\right)+\left(\begin{array}{c}\text{Number}\\\text{of dips}\end{array}\right)\right]\times\left[\frac{(\text{Weight of body in lbs})}{10}+\left(\begin{array}{c}\text{Height in}\\\text{Inches}\end{array}\right)\right]-60$$

To obtain an overall Strength Index you add arm strength to both grip strengths, back strength, leg strength and lung capacity. The complete Physical Fitness Index is found by the formula

$$\text{PFI}=\frac{\text{Achieved Strength Index}}{\text{Normal Strength Index}}\times 100$$

To find a complete photographic description of these tests and the norms of different individuals one must read the relevant chapters in a standard book on tests and measurements in physical education.[2]

ENDURANCE TESTS

If one wants to find out a player's muscular endurance and cardiovascular fitness one can use the *Harvard Step Test*.[3] This is a good test because it requires very simple equipment, no skill, and many people can be tested in a short time. It has a disadvantage in that some people are not fit enough to complete the test, so improvisation has to occur in the analysis of these people. A bench twenty inches high is used and players over eighteen years of age perform thirty steps per minute for five minutes and players under eighteen do thirty steps per minute for four minutes. Each step should be performed every two seconds and it involves rising onto the bench with the right foot, bringing the left foot up to join it then lowering the left foot to the ground and then bringing the right foot down. The back should be straight and the head pointed forward at all times during the test. If the speed cannot be maintained then the person is stopped and the number of seconds is recorded. The pulse reading should be recorded after one, two and three minutes after completion of the exercise and for thirty second periods. The calculation for the Physical Fitness Index of an individual can then be made:

$$PFI = \frac{(\text{Duration of exercise in seconds}) \times 100}{(\text{Sum of three pulse readings in recovery}) \times 2}$$

A reading of over 70 is reasonably good, but for top class international players one should be looking for a score in excess of 110.

MOTOR ABILITY TESTS

If one wishes to test a player's motor ability there are various tests which can apply. Really one is trying to find out a person's immediate ability to play in a sport or event. Tests will include agility, power, hand-eye-feet coordination movements and strength. A simple set of tests are the *Western Motor Ability Tests*.[4]

The first test is for *agility* and it is performed by a player who runs around a course of obstacles as shown in Fig. 1. The player starts from a sitting position and two attempts at running the course are allowed. The fastest time will be recorded. This test can also be useful for assessing power and leg strength.

Fig. 1

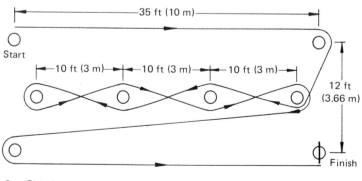

0 = Skittle

The second test can assess the *power* of a player and it is called a standing broad jump.

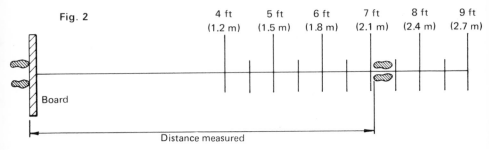

Fig. 2

Board

Distance measured

The player jumps from a standing position with two feet together from behind a board and the distance is recorded from the back of the board to the heel of the trailing foot. The best of two tries is recorded.

The third test is for *hand-eye coordination* and it involves a person standing behind a line, six feet from a wall, and throwing a tennis ball underarm and catching it with the opposite hand. He then continues the procedure so that each hand must throw the ball and each hand must catch the ball. He cannot throw the ball with the same hand all the time. The number of catches in thirty seconds should be recorded and there should always be a good supply of balls available and two trials should be allowed. One minute's practice should be allowed before the test and at no time during the test should the ball be supported by the body, or the feet move closer than six feet to the wall.

The fourth test gives a good indication of *upper body strength*. An area is marked out 75 ft long and 10 ft wide and after 25 ft the distance is marked out every foot. The player sits on the ground behind the starting line at the beginning of the court, with his legs straight and both feet on the ground. A basketball is held behind the head and it is thrown forward and the measurement is taken from the starting line to the place where the ball bounced.

The overall results are obtained on a percentage basis either within the group or better still by a set of norms which can be located in a standard book on tests and measurements in physical education.[5]

There are various methods of testing to assess a player's potential and his weaknesses but I will only outline a few more important tests.

In the *Vertical Jump Test*[6] an adjustable board with measurements in half inches is placed on a wall. The player stands with his feet flat on the floor, six inches from the wall, and with either his left or right shoulder at 90° to the board. He then straightens the arm nearest to the board, above his head and the board is adjusted so that the lowest point on it (i.e. '0' inches) is at that height. The player then places a piece of chalk dust on his fingers, then jumps and tries to touch the board at the highest point possible. Three attempts are allowed and the best jump is recorded.

This is a good test for assessing leg power and the distances jumped can vary considerably. If a player can jump more than twenty inches he is doing well. World-class high jumpers and basketball players have recorded jumps of over forty inches.

An elementary *Table Tennis Test* that is good for assessing motor ability was developed by Mott and Lockhart.[7] One half of the table is placed up against the wall with a 6-inch net above the table and against the wall. All that is required is to drop the ball onto the table and see how many times you can hit the ball above the net. Any number of bounces on the table is allowed and there is a time limit of thirty seconds. Practice is allowed before the test and the best of three attempts is recorded.

BASIC FITNESS TESTS

Another group of fitness tests covering a wider spectrum of activities was developed by Fleishman.[8, 9] The first, a *Static Flexibility Test*, gives a good indication of the lateral flexion of a player. He stands with the centre of his back opposite to a wall chart that is at arm's length away from his body. Keeping his feet perfectly still and pointing away from the wall and with his hands together and the arms outstretched, he turns to the right and tries to touch the wall chart at the furthest point. He then repeats the exercise except this time he turns to the left. The degree of flexion in each turn is recorded from the chart to the nearest half inch (Fig. 5).

The following *Dynamic Flexibility Test* finds out the number of repeated flexing movements of a player in twenty seconds. A player stands 'X' inches from the wall depending upon his size.* He bends down and touches that point with both hands and then touches a marker on the wall directly behind the centre of his neck. His hands move from the left to the floor, to the right, to the floor, to the left, etc. (Figs. 4a–c, page 151)

These two tests are very useful in assessing the amount of flexibility a table tennis player possesses about the hip joint and spinal column. Correct hip movement is very important for the correct execution of forehand strokes.

A *Softball Throw Test* is good for assessing *shoulder and arm strength*. No run-up is allowed when this twelve inch circular ball is thrown and both feet must be on the ground at the same time. The best of three throws is recorded.

A *Leg Lift Test* can measure *dynamic trunk strength*. A player lies on his back on the floor with the arms sideways so that the body forms a 'crucifix' shape. Without rocking the upper body and keeping the elbow joints at approximately 180°, and the legs straight, he counts how many times he can raise his legs to 90° in thirty seconds (Fig. 18, page 156).

A *Cable Jump Test* is very good for assessing *gross body coordination*. A taut rope is held by two people at a height of 24 in. A player commences the test from an upright standing position and then he must jump over the rope

* The distance between the knee and ankle of the individual can be used.

Fig. 3a

Fig. 3b

Fig. 3c

The cable jump

and land, two feet together, while maintaining perfect balance. Hitting the rope is not allowed and the number of correct attempts out of five is recorded (See Photo).

A *Balance Test* can assess *gross body equilibrium*. A player has to balance on a board $1\frac{1}{2}$ in. high, $\frac{3}{4}$ in. wide and 24 in. long. He is allowed to balance on either foot but the non-balancing foot must not touch the board and the hands should be kept on the hips. Two attempts are allowed and on each occasion the player tries to maintain his balance for 20 seconds. The average time is recorded.

A *600 yd Run* is a test which can be used to assess a player's *stamina* and cardiovascular endurance.

For each of these Tests, sets of norms from a wide cross section of human beings can be found in a standard book on tests and measurements in physical education.[10] These tests and measurements can be used in conjunction with tests for the amount of fat on a person. It is possible to find the percentage of fat on a player by using a pair of skinfold calipers and measuring the amount of fat tissue present in the skinfold sites above the biceps, triceps, subscapular and iliac crest.[11] These readings are added together and by simple calculations the percentage of fat on a player can be obtained. There are also social fitness tests of writing, sociometry tests, and knowledge tests of techniques and rules. Once a good selection of tests has been carried out then a coach can prepare a specialist programme for each individual.

If you look through the results of tests I did with the best under-fourteen players in England in 1973 I am sure you will gain insight into what type of physique and fitness each person possessed.* In the occasional case, cheating occurred and this is very apparent and can be detected by looking at the results of the individual on a similar physical test. It is interesting to compare the players' physical ability with their results in match play and then try to form a correlation between the readings. This will remind you of my earlier statements that good table tennis players are not necessarily the fittest but that a good fit player will always be better than if he were unfit.

In the charts in the Appendices, twelve points were awarded to the person with the best performance in a test, eleven for second and so on down to one point for twelfth place. The total number of points gained by each player is calculated to obtain the best overall performance. Out of a possible 228 points, Kevin Beadsley obtained 181. After the matches that occurred at the end of the week Kevin finished only in tenth position whereas Richard Jermyn who finished tenth in the testing finished third in the match play. A possible answer to these statistics is that Kevin was the youngest boy in the group and although physically fit for his own body size, he was lacking in match experience. It was interesting to read that in the National Under-Fourteen Championships in 1974, Kevin was the winner.

While I was coaching the England team from 1974 to 1976, the following report and tests were used on players and I have described certain physical tests in photographic detail. The results that are recorded are those of Nicky Jarvis, ranked Number 2 in England in 1975.

Table tennis report on an international player

REPORT ON PLAYER

1	NAME	*Nicky Jarvis*
2	DATE OF BIRTH	*7–3–54*
3	AGE	*21 yr 6 mth*
4	WEIGHT	*11 st 6 lb*
5	HEIGHT	*5 ft 9½ in*
6	PHYSICAL DEFECTS	*Nil*
7	STROKE PLAY	*Comments*
	a) Grip	*He has problems when switching from a forehand to backhand loop drive.*
	b) Stance	*Good, but he often transfers his body weight onto the foot he is supposed to move in the first phase of a movement pattern.*
	c) Services	*Very good.*
	d) Return of service	*He is off balance when receiving a short service to the forehand or a disguised long service to the middle of the table.*

* See Appendices

e) Forehand and backhand push	*He needs to improve the movement of his wrist so as to impart more spin on the ball.*
f) Forehand and backhand smash	*He needs to make a slight improvement against the high ball which has been chopped by the defensive player.*
g) Forehand and backhand loop drives	*Very good on the forehand. He needs more practice against the counter attack ball down the backhand.*
h) Forehand and backhand block	*He is often caught blocking the ball with his racket facing the ceiling.*
i) Forehand and backhand counter attack	*The consistency in the backhand stroke needs improving.*
j) Forehand and backhand backspin	*Satisfactory. He very rarely needs to use these strokes in a match.*
k) Forehand and backhand flick	*He often plays these strokes without being well balanced so the number of errors tends to be rather high.*
8 FOOTWORK	*He needs to practice the movement to the backhand court after being switched wide to the forehand.*
9 TECHNIQUE	*He is very good at following up his service but he tends to be vulnerable against the player who serves short down his forehand or fast down his backhand.*
10 PHYSICAL FITNESS	*Results*
a) Resting pulse rate	*52*
b) Physical fitness index	*106*
c) Body coordination (Fig. 3)	*5 out of 5*
d) Reaction time	*3·5 sec.*
e) Flexibility	
(i) Dynamic (Figs. 4a–c)	*9*
(ii) Static (Fig. 5)	*24 in. to the right 22 in. to the left*
(iii) Back flexion (Figs. 6a and b)	*6½ in.*
(iv) Hyperextension (Figs. 7a and 7b)	*13½ in.*
(v) Shoulder extension (Figs. 8a and 8b)	*19 in.*

f) Power
    (i) 100 yds   *11·5 sec.*
    (ii) Standing broad   *8 ft 4 in.*
        jump
    (iii) Vertical jump   *24 in.*
g) Strength
    (i) Explosive strength   *9·9 sec.*
        Shuttle run
        10 yds × 4
    (ii) Dynamic strength   *13*
        Pull-ups
        (Figs. 9a and 9b)
    (iii) Trunk strength   *150 lb*
    (iv) Leg strength   *320 lb*
    (v) Arm strength   *21*
        Dips (Figs.10a and 10b)
    (vi) Specific weight training
        Curls   *100 lb*
        Sit ups   *+ 55 lb*
        Half squats   *320 lb*
        Press behind neck   *105 lb*
        Calf raising   *270 lb*
        Reverse curls   *70 lb*
        Bench press   *176 lb*
        Step ups   *270 lb*
        Rowing   *150 lb*
        Shoulder abduction   *30 lb – Right arm*
                                   25 lb – Left arm
h) Endurance
    (i) 600 yds   *1 min. 50 sec.*
    (ii) 3·6 miles   22 min. 13 sec.
        Cross country
i) Balance   *20 sec.*
j) Circuit training
   Number of repetitions
   in one minute
    (i) Star jumps (Figs.   *54*
        11a–c)
    (ii) Sit ups (Figs.   *41*
        12a–c)
    (iii) Press ups (Figs.   *50*
        13a–c)

(iv) Knee jumps (Figs. 14a–c)	*93*
(v) V arches (Figs. 15a and 15b)	*46*
(vi) Pluto sniffs (Figs. 16a–e)	*44*
(vii) Half Burpees (Figs. 17a and 17b)	*57*
(viii) Leg raises (Figs. 18a–c)	*25*
(ix) Arm extensions (Figs. 19a–c)	*120*

11 KNOWLEDGE
a) Rules   *Excellent*
b) Techniques   *Very good*
He is very keen to learn and he watches carefully films of other players. He discusses sensibly different techniques.

12 ATTITUDE TOWARDS—
a) Coach   *Very good*
b) Consistency   *Very good*
   Practice
c) Pressure play   *Very good*
d) Match play   *Very good*
e) Physical training   *Very good*
13 GENERAL REMARKS   *Nicky has the potential to become one of the leading players in Europe if he continues to dedicate himself to the game.*

Signature
England Trainer/Coach.

With the knowledge obtained from Chapter 7, The Development of Physical Fitness for Table Tennis Players, and the information obtained from the tests and measurements on a player, it should be possible to plan an individual training schedule. Obviously it would be impossible here to state a definite number of repetitions or timings for exercises because they will vary immensely from individual to individual depending on their initial fitness. However, a broad training programme should be adhered to.

Figs. 4a–c
Dynamic
flexibility
test

Fig. 4a   **Fig. 4c**   **Fig. 4b**

Fig. 5(*right*)
Static
flexibility
test

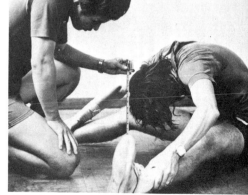

Fig. 6a   Measuring back flexion   **Fig. 6b**

Fig. 7a   Measuring hyperextension   **Fig. 7b**

Fig. 8a   Measuring shoulder extension   **Fig. 8b**

Fig. 9a   **Fig. 9b**

Pull-up

Fig. 10a   **Fig. 10b**   **Fig. 10c**

Dip

Star jump

Fig. 11a   **Fig. 11b**   **Fig. 11c**

Fig. 12a

Fig. 13a

Fig. 14a   Fig. 14b   Fig. 14c

Fig. 12b

Fig. 12c

Fig. 13b

Fig. 13c

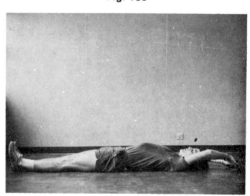

Fig. 15a

Figs. 15a–b   V arch

Fig. 15b

Fig. 16a

Fig. 16d

Fig. 16e

Fig. 17c

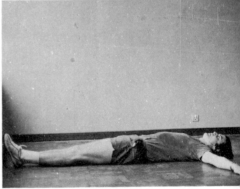

Fig. 18a

Fig. 16b

Fig. 16c

Fig. 17a

Fig. 17b

Fig. 18b

Fig. 18c

Fig. 19a

Fig. 19b

Fig. 19c

Arm extensions

PLANNING A YEAR'S TRAINING SCHEDULE FOR TABLE TENNIS PLAYERS

In table tennis, skill and fitness are very important and the preparation for all participants requires careful planning and self discipline. A good training programme must aim for an extremely high standard of physiological and psychological fitness. A training plan for table tennis will not give maximum benefit unless the player is prepared to change his usual life style and make sacrifices for his particular aims. Really there are no easy ways to train and there is nothing better than very hard work and good healthy living.

A weekly training plan needs to create an increase of work followed by a recovery period. If certain days involve maximum training sessions they should be followed by days of lighter loads. When one is preparing for year-round training, it is appropriate to divide the year into three periods.

The pre-season training period

At this time of the year physical conditioning is the main priority in the training programmes. It provides a foundation of fitness upon which skill can be based in the later stages of training. This stage of training is the most painful. The training load is designed to create the maximum peak for the year in an attempt not only to increase physical efficiency but, through tough and demanding effort, to set a new mental outlook to challenges that occur in the future. Usually only a limited amount of table tennis play is included in this phase of training.

The competitive period

During this stage of fitness training maximum load is gradually replaced by more table work. Weight training is reduced but is designed to create power. The number of circuit training sessions is lowered to allow more time for table practices. The long distance runs used to improve the capacity of the heart and to develop a psychological attitude, are altered to shorter distances covered faster. The training focus is gradually shifted from general physical conditioning to direct preparation for the forthcoming competition. This is done systematically to ensure that the player can gain full benefit from the newly-achieved level of physical fitness by introducing more table training without allowing the fitness levels to drop. The wise planning of training during this stage has a decisive influence on the competitive performance.

Post-competitive period

This is the time after the last important tournament. Players should not stop training, as that would drastically reduce the acquired level of fitness, which should each year be higher than the previous year at the same point in the training cycle. To maintain fitness that has been acquired after the competitive season, flexibility exercises and active sports should be engaged in and time should be spent in correcting difficulties in techniques that were detected while playing in tournaments.

The annual circle of training

Mobility exercises	Daily all year round	
Circuit training; running		June–April
Weight training	Twice-weekly;	May–September
	Once-weekly;	October—April
'On the Table' training		All year round
Match play		September/October–April/May

REFERENCES

1 Rogers, F. R. (1926). *Physical capacity tests in the administration of physical education.* New York Bureau of Publications: Teachers' College Columbia University.

2 Harrison Clark, H. (1976). *Application of Measurement to Health and Physical Education,* pp. 126-45 and 369-72. Prentice Hall Inc.: New Jersey.

3 Brougha, L. (1943). 'The step test: a simple method of measuring physical fitness for muscular work in young men.' *Research Quarterly* **14**, 31-6.

4 Yuhasz, M. S. *Physical Fitness Research Laboratory.* University of Western Ontario.

5 Campbell, W. R. and Tucker, N. M. (1967). *Introduction to Tests and Measurements in Physical Education,* pp. 215-19. Bell: London.

6 Sargent, D. A. (1921). 'Physical test of a man.' *Physical Education Review* **26(4)**, 188.

7 Mott, J. A. and Lockhart, A. (1946). 'Table tennis backboard test.' *Journal of Health and Physical Education* **17(9),** 550.
8 Fleishman, E. A. (1964). *The Structure and Measurement of Physical Fitness.* Prentice Hall Inc.: New Jersey.
9 *Ibid.*
10 Harrison Clark, H. (1976). *Application of Measurement to Health and Physical Education.* Prentice Hall Inc.: New Jersey.
11 Tanner, J. M. (1959). 'The measurement of body fat in man.' *British Nutritional Society* **18,** 148.

9 Kinesiological Principles Involved in Table Tennis

INTRODUCTION

Kinesiology can be termed the scientific study of the movement of the human body. If a player wants to become a really good player, it will be of great assistance if both he and his coach have a sound knowledge of the basic principles of this subject.

A typical phrase used by some players or coaches expressing their ideas is 'Hit the ball harder'. The player may be hitting the ball as hard as he can. What he really wants is sound advice which pays attention to the need for a longer preliminary backswing, a more definite movement into the ball and an attempt to stroke through the ball instead of 'jabbing' at it. This advice has much more meaning and is far more beneficial.

Before talking about the advantages of a knowledge of kinesiology in relation to table tennis, it is interesting to note that players can obtain really high-level motor skills and be international stars without this knowledge. However, as they have never thought of how they execute the strokes, their explanations can be false and even absurd.

When describing a stroke to someone it is necessary to take into account some of the following factors, and form an analysis.

1 Start-of-stroke position and end-of-stroke position.
2 The direction of each joint action (abduction, flexion, rotation etc.).
3 Joint actions (sequences).
4 Joint actions (speed and acceleration).
5 Joint actions (the causes of motive power: eccentric contraction, concentric contraction, etc.).
6 Joint actions (timing, coordination and rhythm).
7 The amount of muscular, skeletal or external stabilisation that a player requires.

As well as these points of kinesiology one must consider the pure mechanics of the type of racket used and the speed, direction and spin on the ball travelling towards you, and the speed, direction or spin that you want to impart. When analysing the table tennis strokes of a player, one should look for strength, power, speed (rate of movement after the start), static precision, dynamic precision, coordination and flexibility.

Warm-up activities
Some players do very few warming-up exercises before a game yet turn in really good performances. Theoretically warm-up exercises are supposed to increase the excitability of the muscles but tests in various sports have still to prove that warm-up activities are of great importance in determining overall success.[1] It is generally felt, however, that:

1 Specific warm-up exercises on the table, or shadow play off the table, or other movements that involve coordination and other educable factors as distinguished from activities of pure physiological function, are more beneficial.
2 Warm-ups are essential in cool climates so as to bring the body temperature up to at least normal level.
3 For non-specific warm-up exercises to be effective it is necessary to cause a rise of one to four degrees Fahrenheit in the body 'core' temperature[2] but one must avoid the onset of fatigue. It is very important to judge the interval between the warm-up and the game.
4 Warming-up definitely decreases the chance of injury in a game.

The ready stance
In table tennis it is necessary to prepare for any one of several possible movements. One needs to be able to move quickly in any direction with maximum speed. A player should keep his centre of gravity over the area of his base until he makes a decision to move, but the area of his base should be reduced in size so that a certain movement in the centre of gravity results in an unbalanced position. The weight is usually moved from both feet to one foot, and if the feet are placed widely apart, the weight-shifting requires a longer time. If the centre of gravity is too low this will slow the motion. Therefore the joints are held in a semi-flexed position so that quick movement in any direction may be made.

Of course, players may use variations of stance in order deliberately to mislead the opponent. Players can attempt to use the head, shoulders, hips or hands to try and make a feint to go in one direction, so hoping that the opponent will play the ball in the other direction. If one uses this tactic, one should be very careful not to overdo it so that it interferes with the final movement. In other words, make sure you do not offset your own centre of gravity, so leaving yourself at a disadvantage.

Terminal positions
The terminal position in playing a particular stroke is vital because it could well decide the success of the stroke. If a player reaches to play a forehand drive but then stumbles off balance, he is penalising himself because he is unlikely to return to a correct stance in time for his opponent's return shot. In table tennis one must remember that the terminal position of one stroke often contributes to the execution of the next.

Follow-through

It is popularly thought that follow-through is a continuation of motion after the contact with the ball has terminated. However, after contact has terminated no action of the body can have any effect upon the path of the ball. Follow-through can be better defined as 'a continuation of a propulsive force so as to increase the duration of its application on the propelled ball as long as possible'.[3]

This can be explained as

$$v = u + at$$

in which v = final velocity of the propelled ball

      u = initial velocity

      a = the acceleration

      t = the duration of application of the accelerating force.

When this formula is expressed v = at, it is assumed that u = o (i.e. the ball is not moving at the moment of contact).

In playing a stroke, the terminal velocity of the ball is directly proportional to the time of application. After the contact period the player should avoid excess motion as this is not warranted by the physical principles involved and will assure a delay in preparing for the next stroke.

Stabilisation

Newton's third law of motion states that to every action there is an equal and opposite reaction. When a player makes a stroke with both his feet on the ground, he applies force equally to the ball and to the earth. Because the earth has a great mass it is very stable and does not move detectably. The player's body moves forward into the ball by rotating at the talocalcaneonavicular joint in the foot just below the ankle joint. Muscles provide a stabilising effect on the knees, hip and spine, and the arm and hand exhibit the greatest motion. At the beginning of the stroke there is pressure on the rear foot so as to attain the maximum summation of forces, and on contact the propelling force is largely applied to the ball because the other parts are effectively stabilised.

If one plays a stroke with the feet off the ground then maximum force in a forward direction cannot be produced since the reaction is against only the body weight rather than the immovable body and earth. Thus this type of stroke is mechanically inefficient and should only be used if correct positioning for a stroke from the ground cannot be played for strategical reasons.

Force

The magnitude of muscle force with which one plays a stroke will depend upon the size and number of fibres being used and the speed at which they shorten and lengthen. When these active fibres are forced to lengthen the result is an eccentric contraction. (Although the muscle is trying to shorten, the resistance overcomes the tension in the muscle.) In table tennis we are nearly always involved at any particular moment with the force of several muscle groups. Techniques in table tennis cannot be analysed mechanically, muscle by muscle, because physiological laws and mechanical laws are not always in concert. An example of this is that, mechanically, a muscle will be most efficient in causing motion when it is at a right angle to the moving bone; however, the muscle fibres are rarely fully stretched. When the angle of pull becomes more acute a more effective force is usually produced. In table tennis the direction and speed of the total body force will determine the force with which the ball is struck. Internally, the bone levers of the body receive their force at points where muscles begin or are inserted. The point of application is where the racket touches the ball. Since Force = Mass × acceleration, the ability of a player to apply force depends not only on strength but also upon speed. The greater one's speed is in relation to the ball, then the greater the effective force will be.

Summation of forces
From a mechanical point of view the main problem in many types of attacking strokes is that of creating maximal acceleration with each segment of the body. It is necessary to utilise all forces available so that the total is maximal. This really involves the summation of forces and, if we presume that all forces come from muscle contraction, there are two basic ways of concentrating the forces from different muscles. The first is by simultaneous contraction and the second is by sequential contraction. The former means that in the action of a single joint, various muscles which perform that motion act simultaneously. Sometimes, however, as in the latter case, muscle by virtue of its structure and position may only be of use at the start of a joint action while another muscle may be of most use at the end point of the joint action. These sequences are usually controlled automatically and subconsciously.

All table tennis strokes involve combinations of movements in more than one joint and all the muscular forces at each joint are accumulated and applied to the ball. The actions of each joint and their muscular forces definitely operate in sequences and with the correct timing and body mechanics the force of each subsequent joint action may be added to give the required stroke.

The joints are usually in a flexed state at the start of a stroke, and if one is hoping to play a 'mechanically sound' loop drive, action will begin at the ankle joint and with a number of extensions and twistings, acceleration will progress via the knee, hip, trunk, shoulder, elbow, wrist and finally the hand. The force of each joint action increases the rate of movement of parts of the body above each joint and a final force is applied to the racket. For this stroke to be fully effective, each joint action must make its maximal contribution by the joints below it being firmly stabilised. This means each joint action tends to end with a static contraction phase. Timing is also essential because if the force of a previous joint does not flow into another joint action, velocity will not increase on that phase. This means the opportunity for providing additional acceleration to the ball is lost. Many players often wonder why they cannot loop or smash a ball really hard. This is often because the initial power gained from the leg muscles is not fully transferred, due to inadequate use of the trunk, hips and shoulders. However, this intro-response timing which controls the continuity of muscle firing of the better player may never be achieved in certain players because the timing may be automatic.

Work

When applying all these forces towards a sound stroke one is overcoming resistance, and this is called work. One gets the capacity to do work through energy and the energy a racket has, by virtue of its motion, can be termed kinetic energy. It is a natural law that energy can neither be created nor destroyed, so it follows that a table tennis player cannot use more energy than has already been absorbed. This, therefore, stresses the importance of specific fitness training if one hopes eventually to improve the force of one's strokes.

'Muscle hypertrophy' is in proportion not to the actual work done but to the work done for a unit of time.'[4] The rate at which work is performed can be defined as power (Power $=$ Work/Time). The more powerful a table tennis player is, the further is the position he can reach in the time available after the ball is played by an opponent. How quickly the player can work will be influenced by his neuro-muscular coordination and also by his psychological preparation. The latter qualities include immense concentration, the will to win, and the confidence to play strokes appropriate to the strategical situation.

Weight

The force of attraction between an object and the earth is known as weight. This attraction is proportional to the object's mass. This means that a person who has a racket which is heavier than his opponent's must exert more muscular force to counter the earth's attraction. Similarly, a person who is heavy in comparison to his opponent must exert more force to move himself into a position for a stroke. By the same token it is quite inadequate for a heavier person to do the same amount of training with the same size of weights. Accordingly, training in table tennis should be individually specialised, and a heavier player should be coached a different game to the lighter player.

Centre of gravity

The centre of gravity of the body is the point on which the weight of the body can be considered to be focused. 'The displacement pattern of the centre of gravity may be regarded as constituting the summation or end result of all forces and motions acting upon and concerned with the translation of the body from one point to another.'[5] Naturally, then, the table tennis player's centre of gravity is always on the move. Gravitational force is continually acting in one direction only, and that is towards the centre of the earth. It will act upon each mass particle of the body and the racket in the player's hand.

Through repeated experiences in maintaining balance, a table tennis player's own kinesthetic and proprioceptive mechanics teach him to be aware of the area where his centre of gravity lies. Proprioception is the recognition of stimuli arising from within the body (e.g. concerning relative positions of joints and limbs). Naturally, then, the more one plays a stroke, the more one learns to regulate and adjust the body to a suitable balance. With each stroke the centre of gravity will alter in proportion to the amount of the body mass which is moved. In playing table tennis the most skilful movements are those which achieve the best performances with least effort.

'An object is in a state of stable equilibrium or rest when the resultant of all forces acting upon it is zero. Unless a force from any direction is exactly balanced by an equal force from the opposite direction, either rectilinear or rotary motion, or both, will result.'[6] During a game of table tennis there is always likely to occur a situation in which the area of the base of support is relatively very small, e.g. when playing a stroke off one foot, and when the centre of gravity is comparatively high (rising to smash a lob). Many forces will act upon the body and they will continually change in magnitude and direction. This applies to all types of strokes and one must constantly adjust and counter-adjust positions in order to maintain balance. In balancing, visual cues are vital, but often in the middle of a game one's sight can become impaired by a particle of dust or a bead of sweat, so one must learn to be very aware of proprioceptive sensations in different tendons and joints and of the messages from the semi-circular canals of the inner ear. It is often a good idea to try blindfold practices without a ball to improve the learning of balance. This can easily be done with 'shadow play'* away from the table.

When one becomes off balance after playing a stroke, it is essential to produce movement to return the body's centre of gravity over the supporting base. Often this counter-movement is too great, so that a series of oscillations occurs. A young person learning the game, or an older person with little sports background, has poorly trained detection and compensation mechanisms, so the occurrence of oscillations causes loss of balance when playing a stroke. The sensory mechanisms of a skilful player will find the faults quite early and then the counterbalancing movements

---

* Shadow play. Repeated movements of the body in a set sequence so that if the movements were made between two or more different 'conditioned' strokes in a game situation, the player would be in a position to play the strokes effectively.

are made accurately in a calculated way, so that the oscillations are reduced (or do not intensify) in amplitude.

A table tennis player must accurately estimate the direction and magnitude of the oncoming ball. The player must use compensatory movements and positional adjustment before the actual contact of the ball upon his racket. Because the ball will be travelling with an unknown amount of speed and spin, a player cannot entirely rely on a set of unconscious skill habits, but must also concentrate on observing, positioning and compensating during the stroke. For success in top-level competitions, table tennis players need to develop a correspondingly high level of interpretation and good judgement in integrating different sensory inputs.

Angular motion

Many of the movements in table tennis are of an angular character because the joints of the human body create a leverage system that permits mainly rotary or curvilinear motion. When angular motion takes place each particle of a rigid body will move along a circular path. The different parts of the rotating body will pass through the same angle in a similar direction in precisely the same time. In kinetics of rotary motion one must always consider torque and rotational inertia. They are comparable concepts of force and mass. Torque is the product of the force and the lever arm. 'The human body moves by a series of rotations of its segments so the amount of torque which a muscle can develop is the most useful measure of its effect.'[7] The actual speed with which one can make contact with a ball is called angular impulse, and can be calculated by the product of the torque and the time during which it acts.

When one considers hitting a table tennis ball, one must always consider the various types of lever systems in the body which allow one to play the stroke. There are three types of levers and they vary depending upon the fulcrum, but we will consider only the third class of lever, where the force is between the fulcrum and the resistance. In other words, the body is the fulcrum and the racket is the resistance. Because the arm is a relatively short lever arm, most movements will involve a considerable muscle force. When considering the body fulcrum it is necessary to remember that 'the axis of a revolving body is a straight line, itself at rest in the body, about which all other parts rotate in a plane at right angles'.[8]

In table tennis the extremities are usually the point of support when considering the axis when in contact with the ground. In a forehand loop drive some turning movements are made while both feet remain on the floor. The body is supported by the feet and the base for the body includes the feet and the distance between them. It is possible for an axis to be positioned between the feet and then move to a different point. The axis of momentum while in the air will stay in a set direction until contact with the ground is regained, so once one leaves the ground to play a stroke, one's initial timing must be perfect or adjustment will be difficult and the point will often be lost. At this stage, we must consider the role of momentum.

Conservation of angular momentum
Angular momentum is the sum of rotational inertia and angular velocity. 'The rotational inertia is obtained by multiplying the mass of each particle of the body by the square of its perpendicular distance to the centre of rotation, and summing products for the whole body.'[9] If either rotational inertia or angular velocity were to increase the other must decrease in the same proportion so that their product stays the same. The application of this law is very important in table tennis because much pivoting and twisting occurs.

When playing a stroke like a forehand topspin loop drive, the mass of the racket arm can be considered to be concentrated at its centre of gravity which is just above the elbow. This centre of gravity will traverse a particular arc of a circle at elbow's distance from the centre of rotation in a set period of time. The further this elbow is away from the body then the less rapidly a stroke can be played. This is another reason why one should not stretch for a ball. However, the table tennis player should beware of bringing the elbow too close to the body's centre of gravity; otherwise one could become too cramped, and in certain situations one should sacrifice speed in favour of accuracy.

When a turn commences when the body is in contact with the ground, the actual angular momentum can be gained in three ways. This involves checking linear motion, transference and thrust. If a body is travelling in a linear direction and it is quickly stopped at an extremity a hinged movement will occur and angular momentum is produced. In certain table tennis strokes the feet are placed in position, and the rest of the body will rotate over the transversal axis. However, in a stroke like the forehand loop drive, there will be movements around two axes. Momentum will be developed over the transversal axis while a twisting movement is produced about the vertical axis. These combinations of movements will produce an axis of momentum which will make an impact with the ball. Actually, a transference of momentum is introduced and this will be passed from a particular area of the body to the whole body and from one object to another. Linear momentum will be checked when a player positions his feet on the ground because of an eccentric thrust action of the body. However, when angular momentum is passed through different parts of the body towards the racket a thrust will be created.

When one is suspended in mid-air and one has to play a stroke, movement will depend greatly on the directional thrust from the ground, but the actual twisting that commences will largely be caused by the table tennis player carefully producing movements through the use of the spine and hips. Turns in the air are controlled by the arms and legs. The relative movement of inertia states: 'The angular velocity of the two moving body parts is inversely proportional to their movements of inertia about their common axis.'[10] During a table tennis stroke one must always be aware of what the arm and body rotation is doing while in the air and have the insight to use the other body parts to counteract movement so the best possible balance is maintained. When muscle groups produce a certain action there will be a reaction in the opposite direction. The further the arm is away from the body when playing a stroke the bigger the reaction will be. The outstretched arm actually creates a secondary axis. 'In reaction, greater angular displacement is produced when the arm is farthest from the main axis, and least when nearest, but the total rotational effect of the whole body remains the same as before.'[11] Therefore it is the angular momentum of the arm about the body's main axis which is significant.

Mechanics of spin
If a table tennis ball is hit so that it spins, aerodynamic effects will make it curve in its flight. The degree of spin a player imparts to a ball will depend on the speed and angle at which the ball is contacted and the adhesion between the ball and the type of racket used. As the ball is rotating through the air one must consider the different effects of turbulence created on opposite sides of the spinning ball. The surface of every table tennis ball is indented with minor imperfections. As the ball rotates in space these imperfections cause a greater air resistance on the side of the ball turning towards the ball's flight path and smaller air resistance on the side turning away from its flight path. A lateral displacement in the direction of the ball will occur and this is what a player calls 'the curving of the ball' (Fig. 1).

Fig. 1

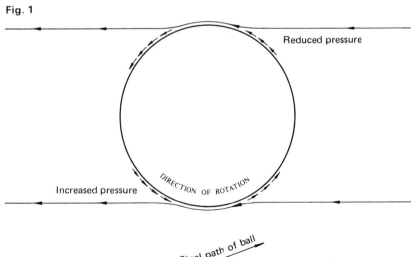

Backspin imparted on a ball

The effect of gravity is a major factor in determining the flight of a table tennis ball because it causes a parabolic downward curve on the ball's path. The curve of a ball with a topspin stroke is increased by gravity and a backspin is counteracted by gravity. There is no effect on the lateral curving when imparting sidespin. The lighter weight table tennis ball will curve much more readily than the heavier ball because of this weight factor. This is the main reason why only 'two' or 'three star' balls are allowed in tournaments. The 'one star' balls usually consist of less material and so the curving difference would be drastically different from the regular tournament ball, and players find the bounce of the ball and its curvature affect their performance.

Generally speaking, when a ball strikes a surface, the angle of incidence equals the angle of reflection. In table tennis many variables are present which will affect this law. The actual angle of bounce from the table to one's racket will depend on the rotation of the ball, the area of contact between the opponent's racket and the ball, the area of contact between the ball and one's end of the table and the degree of penetration of the ball into the table. When a table tennis ball hits the surface of the table, the rebound angle will depend upon the amount or direction of the spin.

Fig. 2 illustrates the effect of spin on the angle of rebound of a ball striking a table surface. Backspin will cause the ball to 'stand up' ('A'). When spin is almost non-existent ('B') the ball will leave the table in an angle very similar to the angle of impact. Topspin will cause the ball to stay lower ('C'). A sidespin will make the ball break in a lateral direction when it leaves the table. To impart spin on a ball it is necessary to have a combination of power, speed and adhesion and to coordinate each set of muscles to work effectively so that they are introduced at the appropriate time.

Fig. 2   The angle of the rebound of a table tennis ball with spin

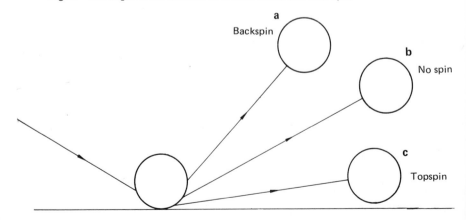

REFERENCES

1 Massey, B. H. (1961). 'Effects of warm-up exercise upon muscular performance using hypnosis to control the psychological variable.' *Res. Quart* **32**, 63–71.

2 Asmussen, E. and Bje, O. (1945). 'Body temperature and capacity for work.' *Acta Physiologica. Scand.* **10**, 1–22.

3 Rasch, J. and Burke, K. (1971). *Kinesiology and applied anatomy*, p. 521. Lea and Febriger: Philadelphia.*

4 Steinhaus, A. H. (1948). *The physiology of exercise.* Chicago.

5 Saunders, J. R. (1953). *Journal of bone and joint surgery*, pp. 543–8.

6 Rasch, J. and Burke, K. (1971). *Kinesiology and Applied Anatomy*, p. 130. Lea and Febriger: Philadelphia.

7 Elftman, H. (1966). 'Biomechanics of muscle.' *Journal of Bone and Joint Surgery* **48 (A)**, 363–77.

8 Dyson, G. (1970). *Mechanics of athletics*, p. 74. University of London Press: London.*

9 Rasch, J. and Burke, K. (1971). *Kinesiology and Applied Anatomy*,p. 527. Lea and Febriger: Philadelphia.

10 Dyson, G. (1970). *Mechanics of Athletics*, p. 95. University of London Press: London.

11 *Ibid*, p. 104.

* Recommended reading.

10 Body Care, Personal Hygiene and Care of Equipment

Do not take it for granted that you will be able to maintain good health and freedom from infection. Recognise that neglect of these aspects of fitness might well prevent you from playing table tennis.

PERSONAL HYGIENE

1 During the summer months and well before your 'on-the-table' training and the tournament season starts, deal with the following:
    a) Visit the dentist and have any necessary treatment.
    b) Try to arrange for a thorough medical check (heart, lungs, blood, etc.).
    c) Have anti-tetanus injections.
2 Develop the following general practices of personal hygiene:
    a) Have a hair style which will help to keep your hair clean and will not interfere with your vision.
    b) Keep your finger nails short and clean.
    c) Brush your teeth every day without fail to help prevent decay.
    d) Take a bath or shower frequently—daily if possible, but always after prolonged physical effort such as a match, circuit training or weight training sessions.
    e) Always, and without fail, wash the crotch area after any activity and dry thoroughly afterwards.
    f) Never fail to wash the hands after visiting the WC.
    g) Give special attention to the feet; they should be washed daily, especially between the toes and this area dried thoroughly afterwards. The nails should be cut straight across to prevent ingrowing toenails.

Try to ensure that you have regular and sufficient sleep. There is no general period necessary for everyone. Some need much more, some much less than others. Ideally a week's trial of no alarm, no call, but just waking naturally (and getting up at once) would show your needs.

Never try to deal with suspected excessive wax in your ears with matchsticks or anything else. See your doctor. Try to avoid rubbing the eyes, especially with dirty fingers. It is better to let your doctor decide if treatment is necessary for abnormalities.

EQUIPMENT

If players take care of table tennis equipment, money can be saved, health maintained and performance will not be affected by external variables. So often neglect, laziness and carelessness lead to ruination of clothing, rackets, balls, tables and nets.

With clothing, a few principles should always be remembered. Plimsolls should be kept clean both for appearance's sake and prevention of perspiration bacteria rotting the material. It is essential that on completion of a day's play plimsolls are not just thrown away into a cupboard until the next time they are to be used. Always leave plimsolls well away from warm radiators or the resulting odour could be rather bad. Try to leave them in a place where fresh air circulates. Before wearing them again ensure that they are dusted down with a suitable powder or anti-perspirant. Many players often wear their plimsolls without any idea of the tread left on the soles. They turn up at a tournament and find the floor is a little slippery. They have less friction with the floor and consequently their movement suffers as well as, or along with, their performance. This neglect of simple inspection could prove very costly in a critical game. It is very important that a player's footwear is comfortable. If the shoes are either too tight or too slack, footwork could easily be retarded. Plimsolls should offer good support, but they should also be light in weight. Excess weight means that more energy has to be expended on movement, even though the excess weight may be very slight.

If socks are worn for a second time, without being washed, bacteria will be present and this can irritate the skin and cause nasty rashes, such as Athlete's Foot. This can be very painful and can lead to distress in movement. Socks worn one day, or for any period of time should never be put on again until washed. Wear clean socks every day and after every training session or match. Thick cotton socks are usually better suited to table tennis than nylon ones.

Change underclothes as frequently as is convenient: preferably daily but unfailingly if worn during exercise, training or matches. Most sportsmen today wear a jock-strap and they are normally very comfortable. Try to avoid wearing the same table tennis clothes without their being washed. This applies especially to shorts. Wash in soap, not with chemical detergents. Rinse very thoroughly and dry slowly and at moderate temperatures—never in front of a fire or on a radiator. Comfort is also an important aspect of table tennis shorts. If shorts are too tight and retard movement in any particular direction then they are no good to that particular individual. They should not, however, be too slack or they will continually cause distraction to the player.

Shirts should be changed regularly. Often in a game one can perspire profusely and even after drying oneself and placing the shirt back on the body, perspiration can still occur. This is due to the body heat not dropping sufficiently. A shirt saturated in sweat should be replaced by another;

otherwise the likelihood of catching cold is quite considerable, especially if the sweat is drying on the body in cold surroundings. Also shirts, like shorts, retain sweat which harbours infective bacteria. It is also advisable to put on your tracksuit as soon as a match has finished. This will prevent the heat of the body from coming into direct contact with the cold air. The actual air pockets between the tracksuit and skin will cause a type of extra blanket where the heat is trapped. It is also good to warm-up before a game with a tracksuit kept on. The body muscles will be 'warmed up' more quickly so that on starting the game a player will feel 'ready to go' from the first point.

In modern table tennis care of the racket is more important now than it has ever been before. Attacking players who rely on spin and speed in their play should change the rubber on their racket after about 60 hours of actual play. Within that time the ball has most probably made contact with the racket over half a million times, so it is quite understandable that the rubber should have lost some of its spring and taction. It often amazes me how players play year after year without changing their rubber and then they wonder why they do not obtain much speed and spin on the ball. It is essential to keep the racket in a dry place so that no water can actually soak into the wood and produce a warping effect. Rackets should be kept well away from really hot places like warm radiators or the rubber is likely to be seriously damaged.

Before playing a game, ensure that the surface of the racket is free from dirt, grease or any other material that may cause the ball not to make proper contact. Methylated spirits on a clean handkerchief is usually quite adequate for removing most unwanted particles from the racket. Be very careful not to use a towel or material which sheds its fibres easily, otherwise the condition of the racket will not be improved. At the completion of the game, always place the racket in a good cover so it will be prevented from gathering dirt. Remember that during the previous game it will have collected particles of dirt from the ball which it in turn obtained from the floor, so clean the racket before playing the next match. When renewing the rubber, use a glue which will allow easy removal but still adhere quite adequately.

Table tennis balls also need to be carefully looked after. Quite a few players find a variety of faults with different balls but if they like one they want to keep it in its original condition. If you are one of those players, remember to place the ball in a solid type of cylindrical container which has a diameter just bigger than that of the ball. Many boxes of balls are too easily susceptible to external pressures. Always be very careful not to store balls in places of unusually high temperatures or the 'roundness' may be affected by the heat.

Table tennis tables are very expensive pieces of equipment, but if they are carefully looked after they can last for decades. Neglect a table and you will be lucky if it survives five years. If it is not an autofold table then it is well worth spending a little extra on buying a piece of rolling equipment like a roller skate so that the table edge can be placed on it and then conveniently rolled to a safe storage area. Many tables now have wheels fitted into the centre edges of the table. In actual storage always place the centre edges of the table towards the floor with the surfaces together and use pieces of polystyrene as supports. Excess dirt particles should always be removed before a game so that there is no chance of an unusual bounce or the dirt being transferred to the ball and subsequently onto the racket. It goes without saying that one should never hit the table surface with the racket (though it often seems to occur with players who cannot control their emotions).

11 Blades, Sandwich Rubbers and Rackets

In table tennis, as in any other sport, a player will have to solve many problems before he reaches a high level of attainment. A major problem is that of using the most suitable racket for his style of game and also for the standard of play that he has attained. When the table tennis enthusiast purchases the monthly *Table Tennis News* or walks into a sports shop with the intention of buying a table tennis racket, he is usually uncertain about which blade or sandwich rubber he should use. Often the manufacturer's guidelines on the performance of each racket, sandwich rubber or blade are insufficient, because they do not take into consideration the playing standard of the individual. This chapter is intended to explain the meaning of the speed and control of the blade and the speed, control and spin of the sandwich rubber.

During the World Championships in Calcutta in 1975 and in Birmingham in 1977, there were many players who were unhappy about the texture and thickness of the sponge and rubber on their opponents' rackets, and they felt they were at an unfair disadvantage during their matches. Many of the points were of a very short duration because the players were unable to assess what type of spin was on the ball, and they made mistakes very early in the rally. Many officials and players began to think that the texture of the sandwich rubber was winning the game rather than the skill of the player, so the International Table Tennis Federation made changes in the laws regarding the racket and these laws came into effect on 1 January 1978. For the rewritten laws regarding the racket see chapter 14, page 197.

With these laws clearly understood a player can at least make sure that he does not buy an illegal racket.

The blade consists of layers of plywood laminated together and as there is nothing stated in the laws limiting the thickness of the wood there can be as many layers as a player desires. Obviously he should take into consideration whether he likes a heavy or a light racket, before deciding on the thickness of the blade. If the racket is too light then he may note that he does not obtain a good sense of touch with the ball, whereas if the racket is too heavy he will have to consider that the arm is having to perform unnecessary work in moving a heavier rather than a lighter racket.

Different manufacturers produce a wide variety of blades, usually within a thickness range of three to seven layers of ply. These layers of ply vary in thickness and the quality of the wood can also vary from manufacturer to manufacturer, and from one range of racket to another. The difference in the quality of the wood and the thickness and number of layers of ply will affect the performance of the blade in relation to speed and control. Through past experiences of playing with various blades, I consider that the increased hardness of the ply, and the more layers of ply in the blade, will increase the speed and decrease the control of the racket in play; whereas the decreased hardness of the ply, and the fewer the layers of ply, will decrease the speed and assist the control of the racket in play.

When selecting a blade, a player should carefully consider the design of the handle. There are various types of handle in terms of length, thickness, width and weight and usually they are designed in one of the following shapes.

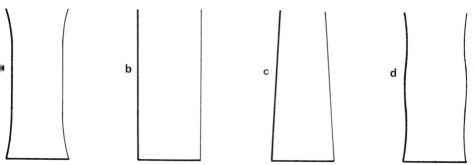

Fig. 1

There is no 'ideal' handle because players may hold the racket differently and hands vary in size. The important point to remember is to have a handle which feels comfortable in your hand during a game. Some people perspire very easily and if the perspiration contacts the racket handle then the racket could slip out, or alter its position in the hand during the execution of a stroke. A dovetail shaped handle as in Fig. 1c or the use of a towel grip on a blade like that in Fig. 1b could help solve the problem. Another solution is to sandpaper a varnished handle or to try to purchase a racket without a varnished handle.

An important part of the blade is the shoulder, that is, the meeting point of the handle and the main area of the blade. Blades have different sizes and shapes in the shoulder area, and not all blades may suit a particular style of grip. The two extremes of design of the shoulder area of the blade are indicated in Fig. 2.

If a player prefers to grip the racket with the index finger completely on the main area of the blade he may feel discomfort in the area of the hand between the thumb and the index finger if he uses a grip as in Fig. 2A. Some players prefer not to have the whole of the index finger on the blade because

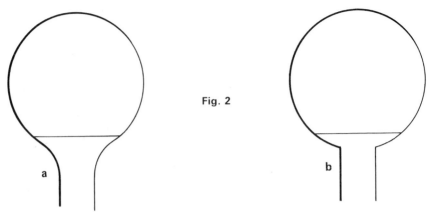

Fig. 2

they want to play strokes requiring great flexibility in the wrist joint; therefore they may want to play with a blade as shown in Fig. 2a.

The sponge on a racket can vary in colour, thickness and quality. The sponge assists the rubber and blade in determining the speed with which the ball will be returned by the opponent. If the quality of the sponge is held constant then the thickness will determine the amount of control and speed it will possess. Usually, the thicker the sponge then the faster the speed but the less the control.

There are various kinds of rubbers that are manufactured throughout the world and thousands of pounds have been spent on developing the texture of the products. The names of these rubbers can be bewildering: Tackiness Drive, Tackiness Chop, Grass Attack, Grass Defence, Curl, Magnet, Super Flash, Bolt, Spectol, Knuckle, Cutman, Spin Ace, Tornado-Tic-Tac, etc. The novice table tennis player most probably thinks he is buying a type of secret weapon. Basically, they have all been specially refined to give their own variation of speed and a frictional coefficient. To assess the qualities of each rubber, a scale has to be devised to evaluate speed, spin and control. If it is stated that a rubber has a great speed, it will mean that the ball will be catapulted off the rubber very quickly. The contact time between the ball and rubber is very small so there will be little opportunity to impart heavy spin upon the ball. It therefore follows that a pimpled rubber which has less surface area touching the ball upon contact cannot produce the same amount of spin per unit of time as a reversed rubber. If the rubber is very fast, then it will allow little control. During a rubber's 'life-time', its catapult effect will be diminished, control will be increased and the maximum amount of spin that can be imparted upon the ball will be reduced.

There are numerous sandwich rubbers being produced at the moment that are designed to counter the spin and speed on the ball and they have a very low frictional coefficient. These rubbers usually provide excellent control but little spin or speed. If a player uses a racket with one of these sandwich rubbers then the techniques of certain strokes will have to be slightly altered to counter the spin and speed imparted on the ball by the opponent. These techniques will have to be mastered by improvising stroke play accordingly. The anti-topspin rubbers, the name by which these rubbers can be collectively described, can be pimpled or reversed sandwich rubber. The texture of the rubber and the sponge and more recently the length and thickness of the pimples have caused great confusion to many players. The frictional coefficient of the rubber was so low that the spin on the oncoming ball was completely different to that which the attacking player had been used to. When a player observed a certain stroke being played by the opponent he reacted by playing a 'conditioned' stroke. However, the amount and often the type of spin on the ball were miscalculated, therefore the stroke that was played usually resulted in the point being lost.

To add further to the player's confusion, opponents began to play with a sandwich rubber on one side of the racket that produced a great amount of spin and speed and used an anti-topspin sandwich rubber on the opposite side. The sandwich rubbers were exactly the same colour so detecting which side of the racket they were using was very difficult, especially since players kept changing the racket around in their hand below the height of the table. Usually these players would serve, push or defend until the opponent misread the spin on the ball and if they had not won the point they would smash the high returned ball with their side of the racket with the sandwich rubber that produced speed and spin.

What was happening when the different spins were making contact with the anti-topspin sandwich rubbers was quite simple. As stated earlier, the rubber produced very little spin or speed so really the opponent was virtually 'playing against himself'. If he imparted little spin on the ball he received very little, and if he imparted a vast amount of topspin or backspin then heavy spin was returned to him.

From all the above information a player must try and decide what racket to use depending upon his own style and standard of game. Only a few guidelines can be given here of what could be appropriate.

Elementary standard of play

To learn a stroke technique correctly one must be able to control the ball. A player could use a racket which produces great speed and spin and it may win him many points very quickly at a low level of play, but as he tries to progress to a higher standard of competition, he will not win points with the same strokes and he will need consistency in all his strokes. Consistency in a player's game needs to be developed first of all, so he should obtain a racket which according to the manufacturer's ratings gives a high level of control and only average speed and spin. To actually 'feel' the ball on the racket is very important at this stage of play because he will realise more clearly what spin and speed he is imparting upon the ball; therefore the sponge and rubber should not be too thick. Although the service is a very important part of the game, there should not be too much emphasis on it in the beginner's stage because once again the beginner could win the point very quickly and so neglect practising stroke combinations involved in rallies. A racket that has a blade with good control and thin sandwich rubber will ensure that you do not obtain excessive spin on the service but at the same time the actual technique in serving will still be practised.

Intermediate standard of play

After acquiring the necessary control in the various strokes, a player or his coach should know what style he will try to develop: looping, counter attacking, defending, or a combination of any two or all three of these styles. There may still be a stroke where he does not have complete control so he may limit the thickness of the sandwich rubber on one side of the blade. He could therefore have a sandwich rubber which produces spin and speed on the forehand side and a thinner or slower sandwich rubber on the backhand side of the racket where his control is not so good. There are numerous possibilities regarding the combination of rubbers on a racket and they will depend upon a player's game, but the reader is advised to keep away from the really thick sandwich rubber rackets until reaching a high standard of play.

Advanced level of play

When a player has obtained a high level of control in all strokes and he has the correct footwork to enable him to move into position to play a stroke, he must consider whether he is obtaining the maximum speed and/or spin on his strokes. Otherwise all the energy he is expending during the movement of the body could be limited in value. If he is consistently placing the ball in the opponent's court but the opponent appears to have sufficient time to move into position and then counteract the spin and speed on the ball then a blade or sandwich rubber that will increase the amount of spin and/or speed may be required. However, he should ensure that he can still accurately counter the opponent's spin and speed as well as impart spin and speed on the ball himself.

The chart on page 182, at the end of the chapter, provides a suggested guideline to choosing a blade, and thickness and type of sandwich rubber, according to your style and standard of play.

The price of table tennis equipment can vary considerably. At 1979 prices, blades can cost up to £11, and a sheet of sandwich rubber may cost £9. The price of some rackets is nearly £25. Why should a player spend all this money on a piece of equipment when an article that costs only half the price may be more appropriate to a player's style or standard of play?

Racket blades can last a considerable time but sandwich rubber, through being a natural product, will become 'old' and will need replacing. An important point to know is when to change the sandwich rubber. Leading players in different countries frequently change their rubbers, especially if they play a game that relies on spin or speed of the ball from the racket. The defensive player who often depends on the control of the ball in his game may not change his sandwich rubber so often, as the rubber is increasing in control with age, but he must realise that the spin imparted on the ball by the rubber will be reduced. Certain manufacturers suggest that sandwich rubber should be replaced after sixty hours of play. At the highest level of play this assessment is quite suitable as the slightest loss of speed or spin in a sandwich rubber could be crucial to a player. However, younger or 'hard up' players, who cannot afford to change the sandwich rubber so frequently, must try and compromise between the number of hours a sandwich rubber is used and the amount of money they have available for table tennis equipment.

STANDARD OF PLAY	STYLE OF PLAY	BLADE	MANU-FACTURER	SANDWICH RUBBER					
				Forehand	Sponge Thickness (mm)	Manu-facturer	Backhand	Sponge Thickness (mm)	Manu-facturer
Beginner	Any Style	Johansson All Round	Stiga	All Round D13 Reversed	1	Butterfly	All Round D13 Reversed	1	Butterfly
		Bengtsson All Round	Stiga	Cobra Reversed	1	Stiga	Cobra Reversed	1	Stiga
Intermediate	Completely Defensive	Johansson Defensive	Stiga	Backhand Reversed	0·5–1·5	Joola	Backhand Reversed	0·5–1·5	Joola
		Butterfly Defensive	Butterfly	Sriver Killer Reversed	0·5–1·5	Butterfly	Sriver Killer Reversed	0·5–1·5	Butterfly
		Toni Hold	Joola	Anti Topspin Reversed	0·5–1·5	Joola	Anti-Topspin Reversed	0·5–1·5	Joola
	Defensive with Forehand Attack	Johansson Defensive	Stiga	Tackiness 'C' Reversed	1·0–1·5	Butterfly	Backhand Reversed	1·0–1·5	Joola
		Butterfly Defensive	Butterfly	All Round D13 Reversed	1·0–1·5	Butterfly	Anti-Topspin Reversed	1·0–1·5	Joola
		Toni Hold	Joola				Sriver Killer Reversed	1·0–1·5	Butterfly
	Counter Attack	Jonyer Standard	Butterfly	Cobra Reversed	1·5–2·0	Stiga	All Round C4 Pimpled Out	1·5–2·0	Butterfly
		Stipancic Standard	Butterfly	Sriver 'S' Reversed	1·5	Butterfly	Cobra Pimpled Out	1·5–2·0	Stiga
							Cobra Reversed	1·5–2·0	Stiga
							Sriver 'S' Reversed	1·5	Butterfly
	Counter Attack and Forehand Loop	Johansson All Round	Stiga	Sriver 'S' Reversed	2·0	Butterfly	Cobra Pimpled Out	1·5–2·0	Stiga
		Bengtsson All Round	Stiga	Sriver 'L' Reversed	2·0	Butterfly	Cobra Reversed	1·5–2·0	Stiga
		Alser All Round	Stiga				Sriver 'S' Reversed	1·5	Butterfly
	Forehand and Backhand Loop	Johansson All Round	Stiga	Sriver 'S' Reversed	2·0	Butterfly	Sriver 'S' Reversed	2·0	Butterfly
		Bengtsson All Round	Stiga	Sriver 'L' Reversed	2·0	Butterfly	Sriver 'S' Reversed	2·0	Butterfly
		Alser All Round	Stiga						
Advanced	Completely Defensive	Johansson Defensive	Stiga	Backhand Reversed	1·5–2·5	Joola	Backhand Reversed	1·5–2·5	Joola
		Butterfly Defensive	Butterfly	Sriver Killer Reversed	1·5–2·5	Butterfly	Sriver Killer Reversed	1·5–2·5	Butterfly
		Toni Hold	Joola	Anti-Topspin Reversed	1·5–2·5	Joola	Anti-Topspin Reversed	1·5–2·5	Joola

			Tackiness 'C' Reversed	1·5–2·5	Butterfly	Tackiness 'C' Reversed	1·5–2·5	Butterfly
Defensive with Forehand Attack	Johansson Defensive	Stiga	Tackiness 'C' Reversed	1·5–2·5	Butterfly	Backhand Reversed	1·5–2·5	Joola
	Butterfly Defensive	Butterfly	Tackiness 'D' Reversed	1·5–2·5	Butterfly	Sriver Killer Reversed	1·5–2·5	Butterfly
	Toni Hold	Joola	All Round D13 Reversed	1·5–2·5	Butterfly	Anti-Topspin Reversed	1·5–2·5	Joola
Counter Attack	Johansson Offensive	Stiga	Sriver 'S' Reversed	2·0–2·5	Butterfly	Sriver 'S' Reversed	2·0–2·5	Butterfly
	Bengtsson Offensive	Stiga	Turbo Super Reversed	2·0–2·5	Joola	Turbo Super Reversed	2·0–2·5	Joola
						Cobra Pimpled Out		Stiga
Counter Attack and Forehand Loop	Johansson Offensive	Stiga	Sriver 'S' Reversed	2·0–2·5	Butterfly	Sriver 'S' Reversed	2·0–2·5	Butterfly
	Bengtsson Offensive	Stiga	Sriver 'L' Reversed	2·0–2·5	Butterfly	Sriver 'L' Reversed	2·0–2·5	Butterfly
			Mark 'V' Reversed	2·0–2·5	Stiga	Cobra Pimpled Out	2·0–2·5	Stiga
			Tackiness 'D' Reversed	2·0–2·5	Butterfly			
Forehand and Backhand Loop	Jonyer Hinoki	Butterfly	Sriver 'S' Reversed	2·5	Butterfly	Sriver 'S' Reversed	2·5	Butterfly
	Surbek Hinoki	Butterfly	Sriver 'L' Reversed	2·5	Butterfly	Sriver 'L' Reversed	2·5	Butterfly
	Stipancic Hinoki	Butterfly	Tackiness 'D' Reversed	2·5	Butterfly	Tackiness 'D' Reversed	2·5	Butterfly
			Mark 'V' Reversed	2·5	Stiga	Mark 'V' Reversed	2·5	Stiga
			Carrera	2·5	Joola	Carrera	2·5	Joola

12 Coaching Table Tennis

Techniques in coaching as related to skills in table tennis
Before going deeply into this subject it is essential to state that the coach needs to familiarise himself with the skills that he teaches, understand the basic fundamental principles involved and be able to diagnose faults and correct them. How a player's interest can be maintained by a coach will vary according to personality, age and experience. His actual urge to learn will be strengthened or weakened depending upon the attitude of the coach, so appearance, enthusiasm, leadership and communication should be good. A coach should not continue with a particular practice if the player's interest has declined at that particular time. However, if a player is really interested in a practice he should be allowed more time to practice it. A coach should also be able to decide when a change of practice is necessary but he must realise that each player may require a different moment of change. However, it is still essential to have a suitable balance both for the group and each individual attending the course. The essential thing to remember is to allow individual flair and techniques to develop.

It is very important that a coach uses all the available time as profitably as possible. If a coach can command trust and respect from his players they will be far more open to suggestions and far more progressive in table tennis. If a coach can develop a consultative, guiding, stimulating role rather than a dictatorial one, the players will feel they are part of a team and their interest will be gained more effectively. A coach should not rely on instruction alone. Seminars and discussions should take place so that clarification of stroke play can be made. It is essential that a coach does not forestall players' questions or answer them too quickly. He should always encourage questions and give assistance to the players in forming full understanding of the modern game. If he does not do this it is likely the players will develop more slowly. It is very important for a coach to know his players personally and be well aware of their home environment and background so that he can better understand their particular weaknesses. It is also essential to notice how the players respond to certain stimuli and to find out what aspects of the game particularly interest them so the coach can reinforce the desire to learn. Players should always be given the opportunity of being introduced to opponents of various styles and techniques, but their ability to cope with these styles will depend on their understanding of their present game. If a player always plays against right-handed counter attackers he will find it difficult to adapt when he first plays a left-handed counter attacker.

Moral development in a player is very important, so it is essential that a coach is not hypocritical and inconsistent in attitudes; otherwise the players will not develop stable and mature concepts. As an example, if a coach impresses upon his players the health hazards of smoking, then he should not smoke, at least not in front of them. When planning the curriculum of the course it is better to have a smooth continuity, with stages of progression in strokes, and not jump from one stroke to a completely different one, or the players' cycles of thought will be interrupted to a degree that is not beneficial for good learning. Therefore do not suddenly switch from a forehand counter attack to a backhand backspin and back to a forehand smash, but make the attacking strokes follow each other so that certain principles adhere to each of the two strokes, e.g. racket direction, weight transference.

When coaching a player who has formerly been coached by someone else, the coach should always be prepared to give a little extra time and patience. This is because that player may have been given certain stimuli which have resulted in grooved responses that need time for adaptation. Coaches should always make notes on players' interests so that if a particular player moves to another coach he can forward plenty of information which will help the player. This can be applied to specialised notes on training, consistency play, pressure play, free play etc.

A coach should always try to create an environment similar to the one which his players are likely to encounter in the next important event. It is useless for a coach to tell a player how to play an opponent on a slow Stiga table if he makes them practise on a Jacques table. It is essential that everything is as similar as possible if the best learning situations are to be created. When guiding players, it is essential that they learn for themselves and not just for fear of disapproval or desire for praise. Players will vary in response to rewards and punishments, the first being more effective. Neither, however, are as damaging as neglect. When a group of players is being coached and a particular player is never given attention, his attitude towards the coach will be poor, and this will create a poor learning situation. It is often the poorer player who needs encouragement and attention for progress to be made.

Learning depends on what makes a person want to work, and this often involves the reward and reinforcement theory. Psychologists have observed that if the reward acts as a 'satisfier', learning will be encouraged, while if it is an 'annoyer', learning will be discouraged. If a good player is rewarded for his success by tours abroad, he is likely to strive for greater playing perfection, but if his reward is only a little prize money for a tournament win, with no international recognition, he could be discouraged.

There are two types of reinforcement, negative and positive, and both play a part in progress in table tennis. A coach might say to his pupil, 'You will not play in the National Championships unless you win the area championships.' This is a negative type of reinforcement. On the other hand the coach could say, after a player has practised hard, 'I will enter you for the National Championships.' This is positive reinforcement. Players will respond in different ways to these different stimuli, so it is once again essential that a coach knows and understands the background of each player so that he can stimulate a player in the most effective way.

Psychologists have determined in the Problems of Arousal and Performance that the more people want something the more they will strive to get it. A table tennis player will really strive to achieve perfection in service technique if he knows that he has no chance of beating a player without it. This is provided the player really has the 'will to win'. He will try many variations of service strokes to obtain his goal, but in time mental and physical fatigue will set in and this will prevent the ideal situation for learning. Learning can be quite simply identified as drive, cue, response and reward.

Verbal praise by a coach can greatly assist learning in a player, but it is interesting how audience participation can affect a player as well. Psychologists have noted that when a player is involved in a relatively simple and well learned task, his performance is improved by having someone watch him. If, however, a player is learning a new stroke, say a forehand topspin sidespin loop drive for example, then the presence of spectators may inhibit learning. Thus an audience impairs the acquisition of new responses and facilitates the performance of well-learned responses. This is why many players do not produce the same high standard of play in tournaments as in match play at the club. Many players are influenced by direct personal expressions of approval and disapproval such as nods, smiles, frowns and evaluative verbalisations. Players are constantly changing each other's behaviour through their deliberate or spontaneous reactions such as pleasure or displeasure, attention or inattention. This is why it is so important for team coaches and players to have the right psychological attitude to situations when one of their team is playing. A frown or lack of attention at the wrong time by the coach could be noticed by the competitor and this could set off an interaction which distracts concentration so the ideal situation for winning is lost.

ORGANISATION OF INDIVIDUALS, GROUPS AND MASS COACHING IN TABLE TENNIS

When organising a table tennis programme one should always consider the facilities and equipment available, the ability of the players and the number of players involved. There are three main aspects of programme planning: The Syllabus, Schemes of Work and Session Planning.

The syllabus should cover all the varying potentials within the group and it should show briefly the type of work to be performed. One should always state an aim and the amount of time available for each session. One should divide it into main areas like warm-ups, consistency play, pressure play, fitness training, lectures and seminars.

When preparing a scheme of work one should always aim for a target of achievement within a set time. Naturally this will not always be reached, but definite targets should exist. Examples are backhand loop drives by 'X' hours and forehand topspin sidespin loop drives by 'Y' hours, or improvement in strength, mobility or endurance within 'Z' hours. Always try to list tasks categorically. Always outline the skills involved in a certain stroke or exercise and explain how to coach them.

When planning a particular session which, for example, lasts ninety minutes, one should think carefully, with forethought and depth. A coach should always know the players' standard of work and he should then keep improving the quality of work performed. Within a session, always have an introduction, a main theme and a type of 'run-down'.

In the introduction always prepare the player for the more strenuous work that is to follow whether it be physiological or psychological. It is essential that a player's muscles shall be 'warmed', the blood circulating freely and the brain working thoughtfully with alertness. When trying to improve skills in a player, it is essential to give adequate time to developing awareness of limb positions and body coordination. It is always essential that there is a balance in training. One should always aim to give a reasonable amount of time to all aspects of the game. Playing continuously on the table without adequate physical training will not create the ideal build-up for competitive tournament play. It is essential that all players perform 'off the table' training for development of all-round muscular ability. If the training is not done, the players will not build up sufficient resistance to the onset of fatigue.

It is essential when coaching individuals or groups that interest be always maintained. This can often involve the personality and personal characteristics of the coach, and his ability to improvise, a quality which comes with insight and experience. One should always have the aims, objectives, and themes of a lesson clearly defined, and when one does this, it is essential that the coach knows the players' practical ability and physical performance. The ideal training camp should have six tables and twelve players. At international level 'two players to a table' should be essential and a group of eight should never be exceeded if only one coach is present. Any more than eight does not really allow an ideal situation for sufficient development and understanding between coach and player.

When coaching one individual continuously, many pressures can develop between the player and coach due to their close relationship. They may see each other for many hours a day for many days a week and, although this is good for quick improvement, the coach will come into confrontation with the player more often. It is essential that the coach really knows the player's social life outside table tennis so he can be more prepared for the personality clashes which may occur. In a one to one situation each must have complete faith in each other. If this faith starts to wane the ideal learning situation will be lost.

In mass coaching always try to keep everyone involved as much as possible. If you have four players to a table and all the tables are being used yet many players are still inactive, you should have assistance from other coaches so they can give certain physical training activities, shadow play, lectures or seminars. It is preferable to have assistant coaches who can help you with advice if there are more than six tables with twelve players, or three tables with twelve players. Some type of rota system should be devised if groups are very large and players cannot be accommodated together. There should be a free period, training period and skill period. The players should be grouped by ability. I feel that if a girl is good enough to warrant a position in a men's group then she should be in it. Naturally, her physical training programme will need special consideration. During the sessions one should make sure that players play with others of fairly similar ability, but they should not play with the same person all the time.

Whether it is individual, group or mass coaching one should not extend consistency play for too long, otherwise mental fatigue could well occur before physical fatigue. One should not continue pressure training for too long or physical fatigue will affect performance.

ORGANISATION AND PRESENTATION OF RESEARCHES, CLINICS, SEMINARS AND DEMONSTRATIONS

Researches

When doing research into improvement for table tennis players it is very necessary to consider the individual concerned. Every person has different attributes and deficiencies, whether they be physical or mental. One should not just look at one player's style and try to copy it. It is essential to look at a cross-section of styles and try to find the style of game which your particular pupil could benefit from. You must consider that it may be a good idea to take different strokes from different players and introduce them to your player. Or you can model everything on one particular player, but one must always bear in mind the somatotyping (classification of body type) of the person, and his physical capacity for work. Also his mental approach may make a certain style of game impossible.

It is essential to take films and video-tape of the best players if one hopes to model a game on their various skills. A big fault can be to watch someone and not realise the complexity of the movement, and without a film one will never be able to go over the full range of strokes effectively.

Clinics

Make sure you know the number of players involved, the number of tables available, the amount of time, and that there is a satisfactory supply of balls and nets. Always plan before the clinic so that everything will operate efficiently. Insist on the correct clothing and always be well aware of what the particular standard of play is. It is pointless planning a programme if it is far in advance, or below the ability of the performers. Try to play two to a table unless numbers necessitate four on one table. Plan the programme appropriately and remember to cater for the left-handed players. Always explain the programme for the day. Before each new activity explain what you want and preferably give a demonstration. Do not over-indulge in excellent performance and exhibitionism, as this can lead to a feeling by the students that they have a 'big-headed' coach. So the message is, never do too much demonstrating, but never do too little. At the end of the day always summarise and give constructive comments for future development.

Seminars

These are very essential, but sometimes difficult to operate successfully. Much learning can be done by groups of people meeting and expressing ideas. One should avoid the formal approach if possible and concentrate on informality. This helps the pupils to express themselves in a relaxed manner. Always try to encourage all types of question, even if the individual thinks his question is foolish or simple. Often, supposedly foolish or simple questions turn out to be very important. Always try to assess each individual and try to find a way of making him participate in the discussions. It is often a good idea to ask people to prepare questions on a piece of paper before the seminar and then to read them out. In extreme cases of lack of expression and confidence in group situations, people can hand the paper to the coach for him to read out and discuss.

Demonstrations

Remember what has been said in talking about the Clinic Stage: 'Not too much, not too little'. Always try to pick someone who can perform the demonstration if you cannot perform it yourself. It can often be difficult to teach points if no satisfactory demonstration is given and if this situation occurs regularly the pupils may begin to lose respect for the coach.

RECRUITMENT DEVELOPMENT AND TALENT IDENTIFICATION

It is essential that a system exists within a country to ensure that any youngster from about ten years upwards has the opportunity to be considered for further coaching by Club, League, County or National level coaches. To do this a coaching system must exist where there is a nucleus, e.g. National Coaching Panel and a 'feeder' system.

The system operating in England

<pre>
                National Association
                         |
             National Coaching Committee
             National Trainer Coach
                      ╱ | ╲
           National Staff Coaches for Area (3)
                         |
           3 Star Coaches and Trainer Coaches
                 2 Star Coaches
                 1 Star Coaches
                         |
                   Club Coach
                  Teacher's Award
</pre>

Briefly their duties are as follows:

The National Coaching Committee

This can vary in size but an ideal number would appear to be about seven. The committee includes the Chairman, Secretary, National Coach, Staff Coaches and the Regional Advisers for the three areas of the country where National Coaches operate. Naturally they have a sound constitution and administration so that every member of the coaching profession knows exactly what is going on. A close liaison throughout the association is very necessary.

The National Trainer Coach

He is mainly concerned with the National Squads, concentrating on coaching, training and tours. It is essential that he attends all the major domestic tournaments so he can assess the lower-ranked players or any up-and-coming individual. He must also watch the different doubles combinations, as often the best singles players do not make the best doubles combinations.

National Staff Coaches

In England, National Staff Coaches are in charge of coaching for a certain area, e.g. North of England, West of England and Midlands, and South East England. It is essential that they have close links with each other and with the National Coach and Panel. Their main function is to travel around the cities and towns in their area and organise sessions for players and coaches, which may last from three hours to five days. They may be coaching basic skills to lower levels of performers or advanced ideas to the best players and coaches in their particular area. It is essential that they see what 'talent' exists in their area and then forward the best players on to national training camps where the best from different areas are coached. The coaches must know the standard of the players in other areas compared with their own because there may only be one from one area, yet six from another, who are worthy of further advanced coaching.

Three Star Coaches and Trainer Coaches

Three Star Coaches usually assist the area coaches at coaching sessions. They have almost the same qualifications but are not actually employed by the English Table Tennis Association. They also take courses for the area coach if courses clash. It is ideal to have one Three Star Coach in each county and for that person to operate as a talent scout and forward his potential players to the area courses.

Trainer coaches are rather specialised in that they are usually qualified in Physical Education as well as coaching to a high level on the table. They can be called on to take or assist any level of courses right up to National Teams.

Two Star Coaches

These coaches also assist in area coaching courses and will often conduct their own coaching sessions within a county. Usually they have a good understanding of all the leagues within the county and ask team captains and league secretaries to forward names of players who warrant extra coaching.

One Star Coaches

These coaches usually assist the Two Star coaches or, in certain counties where there are no Two Star coaches, they may run courses themselves. They also play in the league and look for potential players.

Club Coaches

These usually come and assist in local league coaching, when leagues use their own initiative to help improve their players.

Teachers

It is essential that children learn to play in schools and that coaching courses are held to teach teachers how to coach table tennis. Usually their knowledge is very basic but their job is mainly to interest children and organise inter-school leagues. They should aim to find a local club outside school which possesses a club coach, so progress in their players can be maintained.

This is briefly the coaching set up for the recruitment and development of players in England. The essential point to note is that there should always be an attempt for a close connection all the way from the bottom of the scheme to the top.

13 Proficiency Awards in Table Tennis

To give players encouragement in improving their skill in the sport, a series of tests have been devised so that the opportunity exists for development in a systematic manner. The Halex Table Tennis Proficiency Awards appear through kind permission of the English Table Tennis Association and Mr Jack Carrington, the National Awards Organiser.

Note
Certain strokes mentioned in this chapter have different definitions from the ones I have used in the previous chapters of this book.

HALF-VOLLEY: A counter attacking stroke, block or push where contact is made with the ball very early after it bounces.

TOPSPIN DRIVE: A stroke similar to the loop drive but shorter in action and used mainly against backspin.

CHOPPED: A stroke that imparts backspin on the ball.

ROLL: A stroke that imparts topspin on the ball.

REQUIREMENTS: HALEX PROFICIENCY AWARDS

Bronze Award Tests
a)   All-Backhand Push Control: (From 2 points returned to 1 Target). Using sound footwork for training, return 40 Slow Push Shots (which have been placed, slowly, by Controller from 'B', alternatively to Area 'C' and Area 'D'). Candidate to use only BACKHAND PUSH-STROKES, all played back to Area 'B'.
Required: 40 successes before 6th error.

b)   All-Forehand Slow Topspin 'Roll': Against gentle returns from Controller, play 40 'Roll' strokes, maintaining direction on 1 diagonal only, without increasing speed.
Required: As Test (a).

c) Combined Control: Return 40 slow balls from Controller by playing in strict alternation, BACKHAND PUSH and FOREHAND ROLL, WHILE MAINTAINING DIRECTION ON ONE DIAGONAL ONLY.
Required: As Test (a).

d) Backhand 'Block' Returns: Against medium speed Topspin from Controller return ball by simple rebound technique, i.e. straight-line 'reflection', from the peak-of-bounce position. Maintain direction on 1 diagonal.
Required: As Test (a).

e) Short-Touch Services: (i) From correct position behind the baseline, serve Short Forehand Service so as to bounce 2 times in Opponent's Court.
(ii) As (i) but service with BACKHAND.
Required: In each case, 4 successes to be achieved within 8 attempts.

f) Long Top-Spin Service: (i) From correct position, serve with FOREHAND, ball to land within 18 inches of distant baseline.
Required: 5 successes within 8 attempts.
(ii) As (i) but service with BACKHAND.
Required: 5 successes within 8 attempts.

Notes
(i) For 'Penholder' Styles, for 'Backhand' read: 'To Left of the Body'.
(ii) For lefthanders, reverse targets ('A' for 'B', etc.).
(iii) Two players may be tested simultaneously on one table by using opposite diagonal 'Channel' on tests (a), (b) and (e).

Silver Award Tests
Preliminary: Candidate must have passed the 'Bronze' Tests. Before scoring each test, the Assessor shall require:
(i) A 'Dry-land' demonstration of the ensuing stroke-actions.
(ii) That the quality of the practical stroke-work is satisfactory.

a) Return of Service by Half-Volley: (i) using BACKHAND HALF-VOLLEY TOUCH, return safely 10 Services, varied as to Topspin and Chop and Sidespin. (ii) As (i) but using FOREHAND HALF-VOLLEY TOUCH.
Required: 20 successes (10 + 10), before 6th error.

b) Combining Drive-and-Push, Forehand: Return 40 balls, which have been alternately pushed and chopped, by using (respectively) Topspin Drives and Push-Shots, played alternatively, Forehand, on one diagonal line.
Required: 40 correct before 6th error.

c) Combining Drive-and-Push, Backhand: As (b) but using backhand throughout.
Required: As Test (b).

d) Combining (Chopped) Defensive Returns with Push, Forehand: Return 40 balls, which have been alternately driven and pushed, on same line, by using respectively, Backspin Defensive Returns, and Pushes, played alternately on same line, all Forehand.
    Required: As Test (b).

e) Combining (Chopped) Defensive Returns with Push, Backhand: As (d) but using Backhand throughout.
    Required: As Test (b).

f) Laws, Rules etc.—Answer 10 everyday questions on Laws and match procedure. Points allowed—for complete answer 3; for correct 'sense' 2; for part answer 1. 'Pass' score: 22 out of 30.

g) Maintaining Attack against Topspin from Controller: (i) Maintain 10 triple sequences thus: 2 Forehand Drives plus 1 Backhand Block.
    Required: 10 good sequences before 5th error.
(ii) As (i) but sequences of 2 Backhand Drives plus 1 Forehand Block.
    Required: As Test (g) (i).

h) Service Variation: Deliver 10 services of varying length, incorporating Sidespin, alternately Left and Right.
    3rd error fails.

Gold Award Tests
Preliminary: Candidate must have passed the 'Silver' Tests. Candidate must have the approval of an ETTA Staff Coach as to general level of playing ability and presentation.

a) Topspin Driving under Pressure, Forehand: Play 50 Forehand Topspin Drives, to one point, against Half-Volley returns which have been placed alternately to Area 'C' and 'D'. Good Forehand position and footwork required throughout.
    Required: 50 correct before 5th error.

b) Topspin Driving Under Pressure, Backhand: As (a) but using Backhand Topspin Drives.
    Required: As Test (a).

c) Counter-Driving, Close and Distant, Forehand: Return 20 Counter-Drives by means of Forehand Counter-Drives in sequences of 2 thus: 2 'Close', 2 'Distant', 2 'Close', etc., all returns kept on the same line.
    3rd error fails.

d) Counter-Driving, Close and Distant, Backhand: As (c) but using Backhand Counter-Drive.
    3rd error fails.

e) Combining Forehand and Backhand Topspin Drives: Against slow

chopped returns, which have been placed alternately to Area 'J' and 'K', by playing 20 Forehand and Backhand Topspin Drives, alternately, directed diagonally to Area 'F' and 'G'.
3rd error fails.

f) Combining Forehand and Backhand Defensive Backspin Returns: Return 20 Drives, received alternately on Corner Areas 'J' and 'K', by means of, respectively Forehand and Backhand Chopped Returns, to Area 'L'.

g) Sequences of Topspin-and-Backspin Strokes: Play 15 double sequences of Forehand Chop and Backhand Drive against balls which have been respectively Driven to the Forehand and Pushed to Backhand.
4th error fails.

h) Sequences of Topspin-and-Backspin Strokes: Play the reverse of (g), i.e. 'Backhand' for 'Forehand' and vice versa.
4th error fails.

i) Backhand Attack 'Distribution': Play 10 triple sequences thus: Dropshot to Area 'E'; Backhand Drive to Area 'F'; Backhand Drive to Area 'G'; and repeat etc. Controller returns all balls to Area 'H'.
4th error fails.

j) Loop-Topspin Forehand: Candidate to demonstrate Loop Drive 5 times against chopped returns of suitable length and strength, to suit his requirements. The aim is to show understanding of the 'loop' technique, and a continuity of loop drives is not demanded.

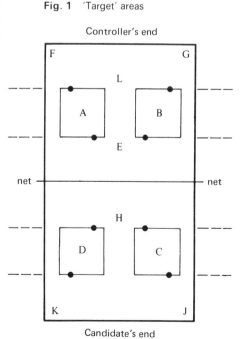

Fig. 1 'Target' areas

Controller's end

Candidate's end

Notes regarding assessment
1 Candidates should be allowed to warm-up.
2 If only one item was failed, a second attempt at that item may be made the same day. If two items are failed, or one failed twice, a new application must be made for a re-Test. A re-Test may not be granted within one month of the failed Test.
3 'Bronze' and 'Silver' may be taken on the same occasion.
4 Assessors are responsible for arranging (a) Suitable Controllers to give each Candidate a fair chance, and (b) a Scorer, to keep count of 'successes' and 'errors'.
5 The 'Controller' should be a player able to place slow and steady balls to required targets, with required spin. Mistakes by the Controller, or unlucky balls, or balls which are not appropriate to the required Test skill, will not be counted against the Candidate.
6 Assessors will rule on quality of performance appropriate to each Test level. A warning and explanation should be given to any Candidate who does not appear to have understood the precise requirements of any Test. A 'Push Shot' is a return which is low, slow and straight, with a trace of Backspin.
7 Appropriate Target Areas are shown in Fig. 1. Since the aim of Proficiency Awards is to train players to maintain control of Length and Direction, the Assessor should require good consistency in these respects, but allow for difficulties caused by inconsistent 'feeding' from the Controller, or difficult playing conditions. If the exchanges become difficult it is fairer to call a 'let', and re-start from the score already reached.
8 Marking of the Table: A, B, C, D, are Centre Points of the four 'Courts'. 'Target Areas' may be regarded as a notional 18″ square. They need not be marked out in full; the dot markers in our diagram provide for practical purposes a sufficient check on the length-and-directional-control of the returns.
Note: Two sheets of foolscap paper can form a useful approximation of these 'Centre Areas' when rehearsing the tests.
9 Assessors should inform Candidates of their decisions and notify results to the Organiser: Mr J. Carrington, 18 Cedar Manor, Poole Road, Bournemouth BH4 9DE.
10 Bronze Award may be assessed by: Teachers; League Officials; ETTA Coaches or Students.
11 Silver Award must be assessed by ETTA Coaches.
12 Gold Award will only be assessed at formal sessions organised by ETTA and must be approved by a Staff Coach or an ETTA-approved instructor.
13 Parents may not assess their own children, above Bronze level.

14 The Laws of Table Tennis

As approved by the English Table Tennis Association

1 The Table

1.1 The upper surface of the table, termed the 'playing surface', shall be rectangular, 2·74m long and 1·525m wide, and shall lie in an horizontal plane 760mm above the floor.

1.2 The playing surface shall be made of any material and shall yield a uniform bounce of 220–250mm when a standard ball, preferably of medium bounce, is dropped from a height of 305mm above it.

1.3 The playing surface shall be dark coloured, preferably dark green, and matt, with a white line 20mm wide along each edge.

1.3.1 The lines along the 1·525m edges shall be termed 'end lines'.

1.3.2 The lines along the 2·74m edges shall be termed 'side lines'.

1.4 For doubles, the playing surface shall be divided into halves by a white line 3mm wide, running parallel with the side lines, termed the 'centre line'; permanent marking of the centre line on the playing surface shall not invalidate the table for singles play.

1.5 The playing surface shall be considered to include the top edges of the table, but not the sides of the table below the edges.

2 The Net

2.1 The playing surface shall be divided into two 'courts' of equal size by a vertical net running parallel with the end lines.

2.2 The net shall be suspended by a cord attached at each end to an upright post 152·5mm high, the outside limits of the post being 152·5mm outside the side line.

2.3 The net, with its suspension, shall be 1·83m long and its top, along its whole length, shall be 152·5mm above the playing surface; the bottom of the net, along its whole length, shall be close to the playing surface and the ends of the net shall be close to the supporting posts.

3 The Ball

3.1 The ball shall be spherical, not less than 37·2mm nor more than 38·2mm in diameter.

3.2 The ball shall weigh not less than 2·40gm nor more than 2·53gm.

3.3 The ball shall be made of celluloid or similar plastic and shall be white or yellow and matt.

4 The Racket

4.1 The racket may be of any size, shape or weight.

4.2 The blade shall be of wood, continuous, of even thickness, flat and rigid.

4.3 The visible surface of each side of the blade, whether used for striking the ball or not, shall be uniformly dark coloured and matt; any trimming or binding round the edge of the blade shall not be, either wholly or partly, white or brightly reflecting.

4.4 A side of the blade used for striking the ball may be completely uncovered or covered over the whole of the striking surface with one of the permitted covering materials, each layer of covering being of uniform thickness.

4.5 An uncovered side of the blade used for striking the ball shall be either naturally dark coloured or shall be darkened in such a way as not to alter the frictional characteristics of the surface—for example, by staining and not painting.

4.6 The covering material for a side of the blade used for striking the ball may be either ordinary 'pimpled rubber' with pimples outwards, having a total thickness including adhesive of not more than 2mm, or 'sandwich rubber', with pimples inwards or outwards, having a total thickness including adhesive of not more than 4mm.

4.6.1 'Pimpled rubber' is a layer of non-cellular rubber, natural or synthetic, with pimples evenly distributed over its surface at a density of not less than 10 per cm^2 and not more than 50 per cm^2.

4.6.2 'Sandwich rubber' is a layer of cellular rubber surfaced with a layer of pimpled rubber, the total thickness of the pimpled rubber being not more than 2mm.

4.6.3 The part of the blade nearest the handle and gripped by the fingers may be covered with cork or other material for convenience of grip and is to be regarded as part of the handle.

4.6.4 Slight deviations from uniformity of colour or continuity of covering due to fading, wear or accidental damage, may be ignored provided they do not significantly change the characteristics of the surface.

4.7 Subject to the requirements of 4.3, a side of the blade not intended for striking the ball may be painted or covered with any material, but if a player strikes the ball in play with a side of the blade whose surface does not comply with the requirements of 4.4—4.6 he shall lose a point.

4.8 Before using a racket for the first time in a match a player shall, if so requested, show both sides of the blade to his opponent.

5 Definitions

5.1 A 'rally' is the period during which the ball is in play.

5.2 A 'let' is a rally the result of which is not scored.

5.3 A 'point' is a rally the result of which is scored.

5.4 The 'racket hand' is the hand carrying the racket.

5.5 The 'free hand' is the hand not carrying the racket.

5.6 To 'strike' is to touch with the racket, carried in the racket hand, or the racket hand below the wrist.

5.7 To 'volley' is to strike the ball in play when it has not yet touched the playing surface on one side of the net since last being struck from the other side.

5.8 The 'server' is the player due to strike the ball first in a rally.

5.9 The 'receiver' is the player due to strike the ball second in a rally.

6 The Order of Play

6.1 In singles, the server shall first make a good service, the receiver shall then make a good return and thereafter, server and receiver alternately shall each make a good return.

6.2 In doubles, the server shall first make a good service, the receiver shall then make a good return, the partner of the server shall then make a good return, the partner of the receiver shall then make a good return and thereafter, each player alternately in that sequence shall make a good return.

7 A Good Service

7.1 Service shall begin with the ball resting on the palm of the free hand, which shall be stationary, open and flat, with the fingers together and the thumb free.

7.2 The free hand, while in contact with the ball in service, shall at all times be above the level of the playing surface.

7.3 The server shall then project the ball upwards, by hand only and without imparting spin, so that it rises from the palm of the hand within 45° of the vertical.

7.4 As the ball is then descending from the the height of its trajectory, the server shall strike it so that it touches first his own court and then, passing directly over the net or around or under the projection of the net and its supports outside the table, touches the receiver's court.

7.4.1 In doubles, the points of contact of the ball with the playing surface shall be the server's right half-court or centre line and then the receiver's right half-court or centre line.

7.4.2 If, in attempting to serve, a player fails to strike the ball while it is in play, he shall lose a point.

7.5 At the moment of impact of the racket on the ball in service, the ball shall be behind the end line of the server's court or an imaginary extension thereof.

7.6 It is the responsibility of the player to serve so that the umpire can see that he complies with the requirements of a good service.

7.6.1 If the umpire, because his view is obstructed by the server or his partner or for any other reason, has an element of doubt about the correctness of a player's service he may, on the first occasion in a match, interrupt play and warn the player of the appropriate requirement without awarding a point; on any subsequent occasion in the match on which the player's service is of doubtful correctness he shall not be given the benefit of any doubt but shall lose a point.

7.6.2 Where, however, there is a clear failure to comply with the requirements for a good service no warning should be given and a point should be awarded against the server.

7.7 Exceptionally, strict observance of the prescribed method of service may be waived where the umpire is notified, before play begins, that compliance is prevented by physical disability.

8 A Good Return

8.1 The ball, having been served or returned in play, shall be struck so that it passes directly over the net or around or under the projection of the net and its supports outside the table and touches the opponent's court, except that:

8.1.1 if the ball, having been served or returned in play, returns with its own impetus over the net it may be struck so that it touches directly the opponent's court;

8.1.2 if the ball, in passing over or around the net, touches the net or its supports, it shall be considered to have passed directly.

9 In Play

9.1 The ball is in play from the last moment at which it is stationary on the palm of the server's free hand before being projected in service until:

9.1.1 it has, except in service, touched each court alternately without having been struck intermediately;

9.1.2 it has touched one court twice consecutively;

9.1.3 it has been volleyed;

9.1.4 it has been struck with a side of the racket blade having an illegal surface;

9.1.5 it has touched a player, or anything he wears or carries, other than his racket or his racket hand below the wrist;

9.1.6 it has touched any object other than the net, its supports, or those referred to above;

9.1.7 it has been struck by a player more than once consecutively;

9.1.8 it has, in a doubles service, touched the left half-court of the server or receiver.

9.1.9 it has, in doubles, been struck by a player out of sequence, except where there has been a genuine error in playing order;

9.1.10 it has, under the Expedite System, been returned by thirteen successive good returns of the receiving player or pair.

10 A Let
10.1 The rally shall be a let:
10.1.1 if the ball served, in passing over or around the net, touches it or its supports, provided the service is otherwise good or is volleyed by the receiver or his partner;
10.1.2 if a service is delivered when the receiver or his partner is not ready, except that a player may not be considered unready if he or his partner attempts to strike the ball;
10.1.3 if, owing to an accident outside his control a player fails to make good service or a good return or otherwise infringes a Law;
10.1.4 if it is interrupted for correction of an error in playing order or ends;
10.1.5 if it is interrupted for introduction of the Expedite System;
10.1.6 if it is interrupted for warning a player for a service of doubtful correctness.

11 A Point
11.1 Unless the rally is a let, a player shall lose a point:
11.1.1 if he fails to make a good service;
11.1.2 if he fails to make a good return;
11.1.3 if he volleys the ball;
11.1.4 if he strikes the ball with a side of the racket blade having an illegal surface;
11.1.5 if he, or anything he wears or carries, touches the ball in play before it has passed over the end line or side line not yet having touched the playing surface on his side of the net since being struck by his opponent;
11.1.6 if he, or anything he wears or carries, moves the playing surface while the ball is in play;
11.1.7 if his free hand touches the playing surface while the ball is in play;
11.1.8 if he, or anything he wears or carries, touches the net or its supports while the ball is in play;
11.1.9 if, in doubles, he strikes the ball out of proper sequence, except where there has been a genuine error in playing order;
11.1.10 if, under the Expedite System, his service and twelve successive good returns of the serving player or pair are each followed by a good returns of the receiving player or pair.

12 A Game
12.1 A game shall be won by the player or pair first scoring 21 points unless both players or pairs have scored 20 points, when the winner shall be the player or pair first scoring 2 points more than the opposing player or pair.

13 A Match
13.1 A match shall consist of one game, the best of three games or the best of five games.
13.2 Play shall be continuous throughout, except that any player shall be

entitled to claim an interval of not more than five minutes between the third and fourth games of a match and of not more than one minute between any other successive games of a match.

14 The Choice of Ends and Service

14.1 The choice of ends and the right to serve or receive first in a match shall be decided by toss.

14.2 The winner of the toss may:

14.2.1 choose to serve or receive first, when the loser shall have choice of ends:

14.2.2 choose an end, when the loser shall have the right to choose to serve or receive first;

14.2.3 require the loser to make the first choice.

14.3 In doubles, the pair who have the right to serve first in any game shall decide which partner shall do so.

14.3.1 In the first game of a match, the opposing pair shall then decide which partner will receive first.

14.3.2 In subsequent games of the match, the first receiver will be established automatically to correspond with the choice of server.

15 The Change of Ends

15.1 The player or pair who started at one end in a game shall start at the other end in the immediately subsequent game, and so on, until the end of the match.

15.2 In the last possible game of a match, the players or pairs shall change ends when first either player or pair reaches the score 10.

16 The Change of Service

16.1 In singles, after five points the receiver shall become the server, and so on, until the end of the game or the score 20 – 20, or the introduction of the Expedite System.

16.2 In doubles:

16.2.1 the first five services shall be delivered by the selected partner of the pair who have the right to serve and shall be received by the appropriate partner of the opposing pair;

16.2.2 the second five services shall be delivered by the receiver of the first five services and shall be received by the partner of the first server;

16.2.3 the third five services shall be delivered by the partner of the first server and shall be received by the partner of the first receiver;

16.2.4 the fourth five services shall be delivered by the partner of the first receiver and shall be received by the first server;

16.2.5 the fifth five services shall be delivered and received as the first five, and so on, until the end of the game, or the score 20 – 20, or the introduction of the Expedite System.

16.3 From the score 20 – 20, or under the Expedite System, the sequence of serving and receiving shall be the same, but each player shall deliver only one service in turn until the end of the game.

16.4 The player or pair who served first in a game shall receive first in the immediately subsequent game, and so on, until the end of the match.

16.5 In the last possible game of a doubles match the receiving pair shall change the order of receiving when either pair reaches the score 10.

16.6 In each game of a doubles match, the initial order of receiving shall be opposite to that in the immediately preceding game.

17 Out of Order of Ends, Serving or Receiving

17.1 If, by mistake, the players have not changed ends when ends should have been changed, play shall be interrupted as soon as the error is discovered and the players shall change ends, except that

17.1.1 if a game has been completed since the error, the error shall be ignored.

17.2 If, by mistake, a player serves or receives out of his turn, play shall be interrupted and shall continue with that player serving or receiving who, according to the sequence established at the beginning of the match, should be server or receiver respectively at the score that has been reached.

17.3 In any circumstances, all points scored before the discovery of an error shall be reckoned.

18 The Expedite System

18.1 If a game is unfinished after fifteen minutes of play, the game shall be interrupted and the rest of that game, and the remaining games of the match, shall be played under the Expedite System.

18.2 Under the Expedite System, if the service and twelve successive good returns of the serving player or pair are each followed by good returns of the receiving player or pair, the server shall lose a point.

18.2.1 If the ball is in play when the game is interrupted, play shall restart with service by the player who served in the rally that was interrupted.

18.2.2 If the ball was not in play when the game was interrupted, play shall restart with service by the player who received in the immediately preceding rally.

18.3 The Expedite System may be introduced at any earlier time, from the beginning of the match up to the end of the fifteen minutes of play in any game, at the request of both players or pairs.

Appendix A
Weight training for muscular endurance

EXERCISE AND REPETITIONS	BODY REGIONS MAINLY AFFECTED	EQUIPMENT STARTING WEIGHT
1 Repetition (power) Cleans a) Squat to grip the bar (knuckles up). b) Up to the shoulders ('clean'). c) Down to thighs. d) Squat, bar bearly to the floor. 3 sets of 10 repetitions each.	Legs, back and shoulders	Barbell, 15 lb Discs 2 x 15 lb Total weight 45 lb
2 Bench Press a) Lie on the back on a bench. Feet on floor. b) Hold the bar across the chest, not on it. c) Press up, fully extended arms. d) Lower to across chest.	Back of upper arms, chest, shoulders	Barbell, 15 lb Discs 2 x 5 lb Total weight 25 lb
3 Two Arm Curl a) Squat to grip the bar (palms out). b) Stand up to have the bar across the thighs. c) Elbows back, brush bar up the body to across the chest with elbows forward. 3 sets of 10 repetitions each.	Front of upper arm, forearm and wrist	Barbell, 15 lb Discs 2 x 5 lb Total weight 25 lb
4 Press Behind the Neck a) Wide grip 'Clean' to across the chest. b) Lift over to behind the neck. c) Press up. Arms fully extended. d) Lower to across the shoulders. 3 sets of 10 repetitions each.	Back of upper arms, shoulders	Barbell 15 lb Discs 2 x 5 lb Total weight 25 lb

EXERCISE AND REPETITIONS	BODY REGIONS MAINLY AFFECTED	EQUIPMENT STARTING WEIGHT

5 Dorsal Hyper-Extension

a) Lying in the prone position
with the thighs across a bench.
Feet held. Hands behind neck.

b) Raise body as high as possible,
while trying to look at the
ceiling.

Lower back,
back of thighs,
neck

No weights.
Body weight is
sufficient for
beginners.

3 sets of 10 repetitions.

6 Bent Over Rowing

a) Squat to grip the bar
(knuckles up).

b) Stand to have the bar across
the thighs.

c) Considerably widen the stance.

d) With the back straight, head
up, lean forward. Pull bar to
chest and lower.

Back of shoulders,
front of
upper arms

Barbell 15 lb
Discs 2 x 5 lb
Total weight 25 lb

3 sets of 10 repetitions.

7 Half Squat

a) Squat. Lift the bar across the
shoulders from the squat
stands.

b) Squat to only one half of full
squat.

Thighs
and
back

Barbell 15 lb
Discs 2 x 25 lb
Total weight 65 lb

3 sets of 10 repetitions.

8 Straight Arm Pullover (Only when 'breathless')

a) Lie with your back on the
bench.

b) Breathing deeply in, take the
bar from an extended position
above the head to well back.
Breathe out when returning
the bar to the extended position.

Chest,
front of sides.
Back of upper arms

Empty barbell,
swing bell or
dumb-bell bar.

1 set of 10 repetitions.

9 Twist Sit-Up

a) Lie on the floor in a supinated
position with the knees well
bent and the feet under a
wall-bar or held; head on floor.

Front and
sides of
abdomen

5 lb weight. Body
weight is sufficient
for beginners.

b) Sit up and twist to take one
elbow over opposite knee.

c) Repeat, but twisting to the
opposite side.

1 set of 40 repetitions.

10 Upright Rowing

a) Squat down with the hands
between the legs to grip the
bar. Hands should be three
inches apart.

Front of upper arms, shoulders

Barbell 15 lb
Discs 2 x 5 lb
Total weight 25 lb

b) Stand up to have the bar
across the thighs.

c) Raise the elbows as high as
possible, so that the bar comes
up under the chin.

3 sets of 10 repetitions.

Appendix B

COMPARISON OF CHANGES IN FLEXIBILITY IN THE STATIC STRETCH AND BALLISTIC STRETCH GROUPS (De Vries, H. A. (1962). 'Static stretching procedures for improvement of flexibility.' *Research Quarterly* **3, 222)**

	(ISOMETRIC) STATIC STRETCH				(ISOTONIC) BALLISTIC STRETCH				COMPARISON STATIC BALLISTIC	
	M Test 1	M Test 2	M Imp.	Signif.	M Test 1	M Test 2	M Imp.	Signif.	Diff.	Signif.
Trunk flexion	10·64	8·76	1·84	·01	10·24	8·64	1·60	·01	·24″	No
Trunk extension	12·42	15·04	2·62	·01	12·43	16·81	4·38	·01	1·76″	No
Shoulder elevation	16·81	18·47	1·66	·01	17·17	19·33	2·16	·01	·50″	No

Imp. = Improvement Signif. = Significance Diff. = Difference

Appendix C

Tests and measurements on England under fourteen players

	Value Position/Points	K. Beadsley	R. Allen	M. Thirkettle	M. Harrison	K. Hall
Circuit Training	Star Jumps	57 1st 12	53 2nd 11	40 9th 4	42 7th 6	31 12th 1
	Sit Ups	25 3rd 10	23 8th 5	9 12th 1	34 1st 12	28 2nd 11
	Press Ups	29 1st 12	16 10th 3	21 2nd 11	21 2nd 11	18 9th 4
	Knee Jumps	59 2nd 11	56 4th 9	58 3rd 10	56 4th 9	51 10th 3
	V. Arches	20 2nd 11	19 3rd 10	11 12th 1	18 5th 8	17 7th 6
	Pluto Sniffs	28 1st 12	15 6th 7	18 2nd 11	15 6th 7	17 3rd 10
	Toe Raises	124 1st 12	120 2nd 11	89 12th 1	96 6th 7	94 10th 3
Flexibility	Dynamic Flexibility	7 3rd 10	5·5 8th 5	6·5 5th 8	8 1st 12	8 1st 12
	Static Flexibility (in.)	5 5th 8	13 1st 12	4 7th 6	5 5th 8	4 7th 6
	Back Flexion (in.)	1 1st 12	7 11th 2	5 6th 7	3 2nd 11	6 9th 4
	Hyper-Extension (in.)	12 7th 6	13 5th 8	15 1st 12	13 5th 8	10·5 8th 5
	Shoulder Extension (in.)	11 10th 3	12 4th 9	17 1st 12	12 4th 9	12·5 2nd 11
Strength	Pull Ups	8 3rd 10	7 4th 9	9 2nd 11	10 1st 12	3·5 10th 3
	Leg Raises	14 4th 9	8 11th 2	17 1st 12	7 12th 1	12 6th 7
Power	Vertical Jump (in.)	12 8th 5	12 8th 5	15 1st 12	13 6th 7	15 1st 12
	Shuttle Run (sec.)	11·4 6th 7	11·2 3rd 10	11·1 2nd 11	11·2 3rd 10	11·2 3rd 10
	Reaction Time	3·6 7th 6	4·0 10th 3	3·2 1st 12	3·3 2nd 11	3·4 3rd 10
	Resting Pulse Rate	54 1st 12	55 4th 9	62 9th 4	60 7th 6	72 11th 2
	Physical Fitness Index	123 1st 12	83 9th 4	108 2nd 11	102 4th 9	88 5th 8
	Total Points	180	134	157	164	128
	Position in Group	1st	5th	3rd	2nd	7th

Compare with match results (Appendix D)

C. Rogers	C. Sewell	T. Stonell	M. Shuttle	M. Harlow	R. Jermyn	D. Newman
43	38	50	45	42	44	38
6th 7	10th 3	3rd 10	4th 9	7th 6	5th 8	10th 3
24	25	18	19	11	24	24
5th 8	3rd 10	10th 3	9th 4	11th 2	5th 8	5th 8
20	20	16	16	20	19	21
5th 8	5th 8	10th 3	10th 3	5th 8	8th 5	2nd 11
55	45	56	52	62	51	54
7th 6	12th 1	4th 9	9th 4	1st 12	10th 3	8th 5
17	22	18	16	14	15	19
7th 6	1st 12	5th 8	9th 4	11th 2	10th 3	3rd 10
16	17	14	14	12	13	15
5th 8	3rd 10	9th 4	9th 4	12th 1	11th 2	6th 7
97	94	116	95	96	109	96
5th 8	10th 3	3rd 10	9th 4	6th 7	4th 9	6th 7
7	6	5	5	5·5	5·5	6·5
3rd 10	7th 6	11th 2	11th 2	8th 5	8th 5	5th 8
1	3	2	7	2	13	9
12th 1	9th 4	10th 3	4th 9	10th 3	1st 12	3rd 10
6	4	7	5	4	5	4
9th 4	3rd 10	11th 2	6th 7	3rd 10	6th 7	3rd 10
9	15	14	14	8	9·5	8
10th 3	1st 12	3rd 10	3rd 10	11th 2	9th 4	11th 2
11·5	12·5	12	11·5	12	11	10
8th 5	2nd 11	4th 9	8th 5	4th 9	10th 3	12th 1
3·5	6	4	5	5·5	3·5	6·5
10th 3	6th 7	9th 4	8th 5	7th 6	10th 3	5th 8
10	10	13	10	9	15	16
7th 6	7th 6	5th 8	7th 6	10th 3	3rd 10	2nd 11
15	13	11	14	11	9	14
1st 12	6th 7	10th 3	4th 9	10th 3	12th 1	4th 9
11·8	11·6	11·9	10·9	11·6	12·9	11·6
10th 3	7th 6	11th 2	1st 12	7th 6	12th 1	7th 6
3·4	4·1	3·8	3·4	4·3	3·5	3·8
3rd 10	11th 2	8th 5	3rd 10	12th 1	6th 7	8th 5
57	61	74	54	64	54	58
5th 8	8th 5	12th 1	1st 12	10th 3	1st 12	6th 7
85·7	85·2	77	107	67·4	82	86·4
7th 6	8th 5	11th 2	3rd 10	12th 1	10th 3	6th 7
122	128	98	129	90	106	135
9th	7th	11th	6th	12th	10th	4th

Appendix D

	C. Rogers	K. Hall	M. Harlow	D. Newman	K. Beadsley
Team 'A'					
1 C. Rogers		2–0	2–0	0–2	2–0
2 K. Hall	0–2		2–0	2–0	2–0
3 M. Harlow	0–2	0–2		1–2	1–2

Beat Team 'C', 5–4.   Beat Team 'D', 5–4.   Lost to Team 'B', 4–5.

	C. Rogers	K. Hall	M. Harlow	D. Newman	K. Beadsley
Team 'B'					
4 D. Newman	2–0	0–2	2–1		2–1
5 K. Beadsley	0–2	0–2	2–1	1–2	
6 T. Stonell	0–2	2–1	2–0	0–2	2–1

Beat Team 'A', 5–4.   Lost to Team 'C', 4–5.   Lost to Team 'D', 3–6.

	C. Rogers	K. Hall	M. Harlow	D. Newman	K. Beadsley
Team 'C'					
7 M. Thirkettle	0–2	2–1	2–0	0–2	2–0
8 R. Allen	0–2	0–2	0–2	0–2	1–2
9 M. Shuttle	0–2	2–0	2–0	2–0	2–0

Beat Team 'B', 5–4.   Lost to Team 'A', 4–5.   Lost to Team 'D', 4–5.

	C. Rogers	K. Hall	M. Harlow	D. Newman	K. Beadsley
Team 'D'					
10 C. Sewell	0–2	2–1	2–0	1–2	2–0
11 M. Harrison	2–1	0–2	0–2	1–2	1–2
12 R. Jermyn	1–2	1–2	2–0	2–0	2–0

Beat Team 'B', 6–3.   Beat Team 'C', 5–4.   Lost to Team 'A', 4–5.

	C. Rogers	K. Hall	M. Harlow	D. Newman	K. Beadsley
Individual Matches Won	9	6	2	8	3
Individual Matches Lost	2	5	8	3	8
Position in the Group	1st	7th	11th	4th	10th

T. Stonell	M. Thirkettle	R. Allen	M. Shuttle	C. Sewell	M. Harrison	R. Jermyn
2-0	2-0	2-0	2-0	2-0	1-2	2-1
1-2	1-2	2-0	0-2	1-2	2-0	2-1'
0-2	0-2	2-0	0-2	0-2	2-0	0-2
2-0	2-0	2-0	0-2	2-1	2-1	0-2
1-2	0-2	2-1	0-2	0-2	2-1	0-2
	0-2	2-0	0-2	0-2	1-2	0-2
2-0		2-0	2-1	0-2	2-0	1-2
0-2	0-2		0-2	0-2	1-2	0-2
2-0	1-2	2-0		2-1	2-0	2-1
2-0	2-0	2-0	1-2		2-1	0-2
2-1	0-2	2-1	0-2	1-2		0-2
2-0	2-1	2-0	1-2	2-0	2-0	
4	7	0	9	7	3	8
7	4	11	2	4	8	3
8th	6th	12th	2nd	5th	9th	3rd

Appendix E

NUTRITIONAL SUGGESTIONS FOR TABLE TENNIS PLAYERS

When I reflect on my earlier years of competitive play in table tennis, I wish that I had had someone to advise on what food and drink I should have consumed. After completing my physical education course at Culham College, I thought back to my preparation for matches and tournaments, and wondered how my performance might have improved if I had followed different dietary habits.

Many players still do not realise the importance of being familiar with dietary requirements; their level of play could be suffering. Young and ignorant of the basic laws of energy supply and demand, I most probably gave my opponents an excellent advantage. An example of my total lack of education in the nutritional requirements of a table tennis player is as follows: I never used to eat during the morning and afternoon of a tournament, as I thought any extra weight would be detrimental to my playing performance. If I reached the finals of a tournament that were due to be played at 7 p.m., I used to eat a three course meal at about 6 p.m.

I hope that the following chapter will help you understand my foolishness, and give you the information that will benefit your match and tournament preparation.

The most important factor to establish from the outset is that there is no 'wonder food' that is going to make your performance improve rapidly. The body can be compared to the engine of a car in that it needs fuel to operate. The right octane fuel will allow the car to perform at its full capacity, whereas a lower octane fuel will cause 'pinking', a reduction in working efficiency. Similarly, a player's overall performance may be affected by an incorrect dietary intake.

The important factors for each player to establish are: the correct type of nutrients to eat: how much to eat; when to eat. There are no simple answers to these questions, as there are so many variables.

For too many years, some coaches and athletes have been convinced that certain nutritional formulae automatically benefit performance. In recent years, many products have been produced which are supposed to increase performance. However, these concoctions alone are never the way to improved performance, and the effect of their intake is more likely to be psychological than physiological. However, it may be possible that certain nutrients are in low supply within the body, and that an increase in their amounts might cause an improvement in performance sufficient to constitute the one or two point difference between winning and losing.

A diet is a programme of nutrition setting out the amount of food regularly consumed to cater for the requirements of an individual. The diet will have to satisfy the individual's basic energy requirements for good health and also for the extra energy expenditure incurred through playing sports like table tennis.

A good mixed diet will normally include sufficient nutrients to keep the body in a healthy condition. There is no one food substance that will provide all the nutrients that the body requires. Apart from providing energy for the body, nutrients are also important for growth, repair of body tissue, and the regulation of body processes. The basic nutrients are carbohydrates, fats, proteins, vitamins and minerals. A well-balanced diet should be in the proportion of four parts carbohydrates, to one part fat, to one part protein, and should also contain traces of the various vitamins and minerals. Each of these nutrients contains a varying number of calories that will contribute towards the efficient working of the body tissue.

It is important that players should understand the concept involved in the 'calorific values' of each nutrient. When the combustion of food occurs within the body, energy is created for muscular activity. The value of each food is measured in calories. (The term used by nutritionists 'Calorie' means 1000 calories, and is, in scientific terminology, a kilocalorie. A kilocalorie is the amount of heat required to raise the temperature of one kilogram of water by one degree centigrade.) For calculations, it can be assumed that one gram of carbohydrate and one gram of protein have a heat value of four Calories respectively whereas one gram of fat has a heat value of nine Calories. For the 'average' adult who is in sedentary employment and is not involved in any physical exercise apart from his usual walking requirements (to the garage, etc.), it has been calculated that he will require approximately 3,000 Calories per day. This should be taken in the approximate quantities of 360 gram of carbohydrate, 112 gram of protein and 123 gram of fat. If this particular adult participated in a table tennis match or training session most evenings of the week, then his calorific intake would have to be increased. The actual increase will depend upon such variables as the length of time he plays, his style of play, his standard of play, and the standard of play of his opponents. If he were not to increase his calorific intake there would be a utilisation of any fat deposits and a quicker breaking down of body tissue. This could result in a loss of body weight and a less efficient work output.

Every individual, whether a table tennis player or not, will require a different calorific intake. The requirements of players will be influenced by factors like age, sex, weight, build and temperament. Young players will require more calories in relation to their body weight than adults, because, apart from their normal daily requirements, including playing table tennis, they need food to assist growth. If a person is under-nourished in his early years, it is possible that complications could develop in achieving a correct feeding pattern during adolescence. Throughout life, males usually require more food than females, but a girl's adolescent growth spurt occurs earlier than a boy's, so there must be a suitable increase in her calorific intake during this stage of life. In a boy's adolescent growth spurt, especially between the years of sixteen and eighteen, there is a rapid growth and development of the body. During adolescence, players should have an increased intake of protein to assist in the development of muscle tissue. Between the ages of nineteen and twenty, a male often requires more food than an adult male, and a female will require approximately the same amount as the adult male. After the adolescent period, growth will continue only marginally, but correct feeding is necessary for muscular development.

Players of the same age may vary considerably in their weight or build; a heavier person should be aware that he will require a higher calorific intake than a person who is lighter in weight, if he is to make the same amount of movements in a game.

Some people become very nervous in competition, and may spend several hours worrying about a particular match. This nervous tension will bring about an increased demand upon the body and an increase in calorific requirements.

Although a person needs to increase his calorific intake if he is playing a sport like table tennis, it does not necessarily follow, if an extra hundred Calories are required per day, that they should be taken in the same proportions as the normal mixed diet that was recommended for a sedentary worker. There is a school of thought which believes that the overall proportions of nutrient intake should be altered so as to prepare for a particular event.

Although my ideas of what is the correct proportion for a tournament are based on previous experience, there are international players who have turned in remarkable performances on very unusual diets. Some players eat huge quantities of meat; others may be vegetarians; some reduce their fat calorific intake while others make no change in the balance of normal mixed diet. When playing in tournaments abroad, many players eat anything that is served to them.

I will now try to explain a scientific approach to preparation for a major event. (One must, however, bear in mind that no exact chart has ever been designed; in this field of study, men seem at times to be able to defy science.)

Proteins are essential to the body but not for the purpose that many players think, which is that of giving an immediate store of energy. How often have you heard athletes mention that they have eaten a large steak, to prepare themselves for a particular match, or heard of a manager having taken out his team for a meal consisting of a platter of steak so that the players will be well prepared for a match? It would be more apt for this type of meal to be eaten after a tournament. The relatively high protein content of steak in relation to many other foods is primarily used for replacing the body tissues that have been broken down during intense match play. During heavy exercise a player on a normal mixed diet will initially obtain energy from carbohydrate stores, then from fat stores, and finally, if these other supplies become extremely low, from protein stores. During most table tennis matches a player will never utilise protein stores. For energy to be easily released for muscular contraction it is the amount of carbohydrate and fat stores readily available that are most important. **Carbohydrates** are stored in the liver as glycogen and converted to glucose (by chemical processes that need not concern us here) and transported to the muscle tissue to replenish glycogen stores that are being used during repeated muscle contraction. **Fats** are stored in deposits in the liver and body spaces and they are converted to nonesterified acids and glycerol, both of which can be easily utilised as a source of energy for muscular contraction. Although one gram of fat will release nine Calories of energy in comparison with the four Calories per gram of carbohydrate, the combustion of carbohydrate stores releases 25 per cent more calories per litre of oxygen than that of fat stores.[1] Actually, carbohydrates and fats are used together to contribute to an energy source, but a greater percentage of carbohydrate usage is preferable.

The glycogen store of a muscle is mainly responsible for the continuation of strenuous exercise in a muscle,[2] and can also assist in muscular endurance.[3] The actual glycogen content can be increased by changing the diet. A diet consisting of a high level of fat plus protein – meat, eggs, bacon, butter and a little salad – will produce a low muscle-glycogen content of about 6g/kg of muscle. A diet very high in carbohydrate content – bread, potatoes, sugar, fruit and juices – can increase the glycogen content to 47g/kg of muscle.[4, 5] Considering this information, a player would be wise to base a pre-competition diet on a high intake of carbohydrates and then, just prior to the event, to top up with glucose.

Astrand offers the following suggestions on how to obtain the best assistance from a dietary intake before an event. The preparation should consist of depleting the glycogen stores in muscle by exercise, then using a diet high in fat and protein, and then transferring to a high carbohydrate diet for the two or three days before the actual event.[6] In the last few days before the event, strenuous exercise should be avoided so as not to decrease the optimum glycogen stores.

Investigations in East Germany[7] classify table tennis as a sport with a pronounced demand on reaction and strength over short periods of time. It was calculated that players with an average body weight of 74 kg required an optimal intake of 4,895 Calories per day. It was also calculated that a yachtsman and footballer of the same weight would require a daily intake of 5,170 and 5,885 Calories respectively. It is my opinion that the figures for the table tennis player are rather low, especially if the player is involved in a tournament for a whole day. However, if we use the figure of 4,895 Calories, another set of figures can be produced to assist a player with his dietary preparation for a tournament. Eighty hours before a tournament a player should base his diet on a proportion of 45 per cent carbohydrate, 35 per cent fat and 20 per cent protein:

> 2,203 Calories from carbohydrates
> 1,713 Calories from fats
> 979 Calories from proteins.

The heat-value concept dictates that the following amounts of food would need to be consumed:

> 550 gram of carbohydrate
> 190 gram of fat
> 245 gram of protein.

When we know that the player weighs 74 kg we therefore know that he would need to eat a certain number of gram per kilogram of body weight:

> 7·44 gram of carbohydrate
> 2·57 gram of fat
> 3·31 gram of protein.

Forty-eight hours before a tournament, a player should change his diet to 70 per cent carbohydrate, 20 per cent fat and 10 per cent protein:

> 3,427 Calories from carbohydrate
> 979 Calories from fat
> 489 Calories from protein.

Using the heat-value concept, this is equivalent to:

> 857 gram of carbohydrate
> 109 gram of fat
> 122 gram of protein.

This gives these figures for gram per kilogram of body weight:

> 11·58 gram of carbohydrate
> 1·47 gram of fat
> 1·65 gram of protein.

Therefore we can calculate how many calories of each type of basic nutrient a player of a given weight will need to eat. For example, the following figures are for a 60 kg player.

(Player's   ×   (Gram per kg   ×   (Heat value per =   (Calorie
weight)   body weight)   gram in Calories)   intake)

Eighty hours before an event:

carbohydrates	$60 \times 7{\cdot}44$	$\times 4$	$= 1785{\cdot}6$
fats	$60 \times 2{\cdot}57$	$\times 9$	$= 1387{\cdot}8$
proteins	$60 \times 3{\cdot}31$	$\times 4$	$= 794{\cdot}4$
			$3967{\cdot}8$

A diet, forty hours before an event:

carbohydrates	$60 \times 11{\cdot}58$	$\times 4$	$= 2779{\cdot}2$
fats	$60 \times 1{\cdot}47$	$\times 9$	$= 793{\cdot}8$
proteins	$60 \times 1{\cdot}65$	$\times 4$	$= 396{\cdot}0$
			$3968{\cdot}0$

Research by Green and Thomas[8] has indicated that an intake of glucose can cause the most rapid replacement or supplement of fuel for muscular contraction. Within twenty minutes, there can be a considerable increase in blood glucose concentration. It will be more beneficial if this extra glucose is taken before the level of blood glucose becomes very low (hypoglycaemia) and it is better taken in a syrup solution rather than in a powder form. When playing in a tournament it is important that a player studies his playing schedule very carefully and then he can plan his schedule of glucose intake.

The timing of meals before a major event can have an effect upon a player's performance. If a county or international fixture is due to start at 7 p.m., then a careful dietary intake should be considered by the players. The pre-game meal should be taken at least two hours earlier, and it should not be too bulky. A player wants most of the food to have left his stomach before he starts play, so that larger volumes of blood are available to assist in muscular activity, instead of being directed to the alimentary tract to aid digestion. In the pre-game meal certain foods should be avoided: spiced foods, onions, baked beans, apples, and cabbage. Also to be avoided are fatty foods, because they are not as efficient to break down into energy, and high protein foods, because of the possible effect of acidosis.

Listed below are examples of foods high in carbohydrates, fats and proteins:

carbohydrates	bread, cereals, milk, sugar, potatoes, honey, spaghetti, fruit
fat	butter, meat, whole milk, nuts, bacon, cream oils, avocados, margarine
protein	meat, dairy foods, cereals, milk, nuts eggs, fish, vegetables

It has previously been stated that carbohydrates and fats are mainly needed to supply energy, whereas proteins are mainly concerned with growth and repair. However, the quality of protein is very important. Proteins are broken down into amino acids during digestion. Altogether there are 23 amino acids. 13 can be internally synthesised from other amino acids ingested. The other 10 must be taken in the diet and are therefore called essential amino acids. Proteins are graded on the basis of whether they include all the essential amino acids. Those that do—meat and animal products—are called 'first class' proteins; whereas those that do not—most vegetables—are called 'second class' proteins. It is therefore desirable that the intake of animal protein be greater than that of vegetable protein. However, if one is a vegetarian, it is possible to obtain all the essential amino acids by eating a wide range of vegetable products.

One must try to eat products that also include adequate supplies of different vitamins and minerals; these are important for growth, repair and regulation of body processes.

Vitamins are an essential part of the diet. There are usually sufficient vitamins in a normal mixed diet and if a person increases his daily rate of energy expenditure by playing table tennis then the relative increase in the amount of food he consumes should be sufficient to meet his vitamin requirements. An amount of a vitamin in excess of what the body requires during physical exercise is usually excreted from the body, and additional intake has no advantageous effects upon performance. If certain vitamins are not supplemented in the diet before heavy exercise then the performer's capabilities can suffer.[9] These observations were made by an Austrian physiologist, Prokop; he stressed the importance of vitamin C and E supplementation, and the need for balance between certain vitamins (B1, B2, B6, C and E).

Increases in the B vitamins are necessary because these vitamins assist in carbohydrate metabolism. Vitamin C is closely associated with adrenal metabolism; vitamin E can influence the amount of stress involved in heavy muscular exercise.[10]

Various minerals are involved in assisting the body's regulatory processes and in the growth and repair of bone and tissue. If the various minerals are not supplied in the correct proportions, detrimental effects can occur. However, as with vitamins, it seems that there is no improvement in physical performance by overloading the body with quantities of minerals in excess of the body's needs. A good mixed diet, and an increase in food consumption in relation to work performed, should cater for the individual's needs.

The most important factor that a player should consider, regarding minerals, is the saltwater balance within the body. Research by Vaughn Thomas[11] has shown that a sportsman may lose over 2·5 litres of water through sweating in an hour, and 9 litres in 5 hours. This loss of liquid will make a player thirsty. He should continually replace it, or signs of dehydration, and a lowering of performance will soon occur. Sodium and chloride ion concentrations are seriously affected by sweat loss, and unless these concentrations are maintained, by ingesting salt, cramps can occur. Therefore, it is essential not just to drink water to replace sweat but to drink a liquid with a similar salt concentration as sweat (0·2 per cent). During a tournament it would be beneficial for players to ensure that they increase their level of salt intake on the food they consume as this form of salt intake is usually more palatable to the individual than drinking a salt solution or swallowing salt tablets.

Different vitamins and minerals can be found in the following foods, and water is contained in almost all foods.

Vitamins

vitamin A	liver, butter, egg yolk, tomatoes, kidney, dark green and deep yellow vegetables and fruit
vitamin B	yeast, liver, pork, cereals, cheese, milk, potatoes
vitamin C	citrus fruits, tomatoes, cabbage, potatoes, strawberries
vitamin D	fish oils, herring, salmon, butter, margarine
vitamin E	wheat germ, egg yolk, beef liver, cereals
vitamin K	spinach, cabbage, fat, cauliflower, egg yolk, cress

Minerals

calcium	milk, cheese, herring, cabbage, lettuce, sardines, bread, egg
copper	liver, beef, bread, fish (general mixed diet)
iodine	sea foods, vegetables grown in iodine rich soils
iron	eggs, liver, enriched bread, cereals
manganese	liver, peas, bread, fish (general mixed diet)
magnesium	cereals, vegetables, table salt, fruits
phosphorus	dairy products, milk, most proteins
potassium	cereals, fruit, vegetables, table salt
sodium	table salt, bread, milk (general mixed diet)

REFERENCES
1 Johnson, P. B., Updyke, W. F., Stolberg, D. C. and Schaefer, M. (1966). *Physical Education. A problem-solving approach to health and fitness*, p. 202, Holt, Rinehart and Winston: New York.
2 Hermansen, L., Hultman, E., and Saltin, B. (1967). 'Muscle glycogen during prolonged severe exercise.' *Acta Physiol. Scand.*, **71**, 140.
3 Karlsson, J., and Saltin, B. (1971). 'Diet, muscle glycogen and endurance performance.' *J. Appl. Physiol.* **31**, 203.
4 Bergstrom, J., Hermansen, L., Hultman, E., and Saltin, B. (1967). 'Diet, muscle

glycogen and physical performance.' *Acta Physiol. Scand.* **71**, 140.
5 Hultman, E., and Bergstrom. J. (1967). 'Muscle glycogen synthesis in relation to diet studies in normal subjects.' *Acta Med. Scand.* **182**, 109.
6 Astrand, P.–O. (1967). 'Diet and athletic performance.' *Fedn Proc. Fedn Am. Socs. Exp. Biol.* **26**, 1772.
7 Grate, H. K. (1964). *Optimate Ernahrungsbilanzen für heistungs sportler.* Akademic-Verlag: Berlin.
8 Green, L. F., and Thomas, V. (1971). 'Some effects of glucose syrup ingestion during vigorous exercise of differing intensities and durations.' *Proceedings of the Nutrition Society* **31**, 5A.
9 Prokop, L. (1965). 'Vitamins and sports performance.' *Periodical for Nutritional Research* (Supplement 4). Steinkopf: Darmstadt.
10 Williams, J. G. P., Sperryn, P. N. (1976). *Sports medicine*, pp. 227–8. Edward Arnold (Publishers) Limited: London.*
11 Thomas, V. (1975). *Exercise physiology*, p. 158. Crosby Lockwood Staples: St. Albans.

* Recommended reading

Index